Journalism and the Media

An Introduction to Mass Communications

by Donald H. Johnston
Columbia University

 **BARNES & NOBLE BOOKS**

A DIVISION OF HARPER & ROW, PUBLISHERS

New York, Hagerstown, San Francisco, London

Contents

Contents

Journalism and the Media

Introduction

In the final quarter of the twentieth century, American journalism and the mass media are generating more public interest than ever before. They are caught up in an information and communications revolution. The press has been stimulated by the role it played in the Watergate scandal. The investigative reporter has become a sort of folk hero. Journalism schools are experiencing unprecedented popularity.

The press, as the news media are commonly called, acts as surrogate for the American people by providing information on which they base their decisions. It is a profitable industry that enjoys a unique constitutional protection. It is a social and political force quite unmatched anywhere in an increasingly complicated world. And because the news system in the United States is so pervasive, versatile, and powerful, there is continuous debate about its performance, its methods, its responsibilities, and its influence in the gathering and presentation of news.

Yet, historically there has been much misunderstanding of the news media, and ignorance of the principles and traditions on which their practices are based. Henry Grunwald, in a *Time* magazine essay, has described the confusing nature of the press as follows:

> It is a profitmaking enterprise, but it is not judged chiefly by commercial success. It performs a public service, but it is neither regulated nor licensed. Journalists have considerable power to help or hurt, but there is no code, no professional association to judge their performance. Paradoxical though all this may appear, it simply means that the American press is free—and would lose all its value to the country if it were otherwise.[1]

Journalism and the Media is an introduction to the news system. It is not intended as a comprehensive description and analysis of mass communications; rather, it is an outline survey of the functions, history, and operations of the media, and the techniques used by journalists to gather, write, and present the news. The hope is that the book will assist the reader in sorting out the essential aspects of the news system and thus promote better understanding of a powerful institution.

The responsibility imposed on the journalist and the media is greater today than ever before. "Knowable" news is continually expanding because of new electronic "information machines" that increase both the availability and the transmission of information. The journalist is the liaison, the link, between the people and their leaders and society's specialists: it is the journalist's job to make complicated issues understandable to the average person. The media, as purveyors of information, largely determine the agenda of public discussion through their selection of news to include in publications and broadcasts.

In common usage the terms "journalism," "media," and "press" tend to be lumped together and used interchangeably. Strictly defined, the terms have different meanings. "Journalism" is the *process* of gathering, selecting, interpreting, and disseminating news. The "media" are the *means*—the forms of communication and the organizations that operate them—by which the journalistic process is carried out. The "press" technically denotes the newspapers only, but its meaning has been stretched to cover any news operation in the print and broadcast media. (The term "press" traces back to the mid-fifteenth century when Johann Gutenberg designed his printing press with movable type. The device, which began a revolution in man's ability to communicate, was a converted wine press that pressed inked type against paper in the manner that grape was pressed against grape.)

The term "mass media," in common usage, tends to be interpreted as including virtually any publication, broadcast program, book, or film, regardless of the size and type of audience for which it is intended. "Mass communications" covers all the mass media plus some other communications forms such as the telephone and telegraph, the postal service, and electronic financial transactions systems. This book concentrates on the media that deal with the news—newspapers and newsmagazines, and radio and television.

Since the beginning of the nation, the press has received special attention as a watchdog of the public interest. Thomas Jefferson, noting that public opinion was the basis of American government, observed: "Were it left to me to decide whether we should have a government without newspapers, or newspapers without a government, I should not hesitate a moment to prefer the latter."

The media in the United States are basically a commercial and private-enterprise system, and they are probably as free of government control as any other system in the world. In this respect, they differ from the government-controlled media in the Soviet Union and China, for example, and the systems in many other nations that are under mixed government, public, and private control.

Contrary to a widely held belief, the American news media are far from being monolithic. They are diverse in both ownership and intellectual attitudes. Although the products of the various segments of the media—such as newspapers—are generally similar in form and content, the media nevertheless are operated for the most part independently of one another in accordance with the wishes of their owners. Similarly, journalists as a group have traits in common, but they also have individual tastes and values that induce varying treatments of news.

Essentially the news media both mirror society and influence it. They develop through close interaction with the political, social, economic, and intellectual environments. Historically, new communications forms—printing press, telegraph, telephone, radio, television, computer—have altered cultures and traditional assumptions. Television, for example, is considered to have had great impact on the directions taken by the civil-rights and student movements in the 1960s.

But while it seems clear that the media in an open society influence the thinking and behavior of the public and government officials, it is perhaps less evident that the public, as consumers, helps shape the media and the content of what they offer. News is a commercial commodity subject to marketplace practices and competition.

By the 1970s, the American media were flourishing. Paradoxically, as a mass institution, they also were on the defensive against criticism—a reflection of the reality that it is impossible to satisfy everyone in a heterogeneous, open society. The news media were accused of excessive sensationalism, distortion, trivialization, and bias, and of restricting access to information and its outlets. They were challenged on the legality of some of their methods and threatened with cutbacks in the First Amendment freedom. They were chastised for bearing bad tidings.

A strong public curiosity about the press has always existed, probably because of the special place it has in American society. Also, there has been a lingering "romantic" image of the reporter as someone "close to the action" recording "history as it happens"—an image that overlooks the routine and tedious in a journalist's work. There is less romanticizing in today's world of televised news conferences and computerized newsrooms, but serious interest in the media as an institution has nevertheless grown sharply.

A major reason for the interest is the rapid change in society that produces new reactions from the media. Another is the increasing ubiquity of the media, making any controversy surrounding them more visibly evident.

Still another reason, perhaps, is that the press's role has been shifting in some major, significant stories from purely passive to occasionally active. Reporters in some instances are not only recording events; they are involved in them. This was true, for example, of the civil-rights movement story, the youth unrest of the 1960s, and the Vietnam War. And it certainly was most dramatically true of the historic Watergate episode, as investigative work by the news media contributed extensively to revelations of government ills and excesses that led to the downfall of Richard M. Nixon, the first American President to resign from office.

The press has had its special place in American society since it was given its First Amendment protection by the framers of the Constitution. Its purpose has been to keep the people informed, based on the proposition that an informed people could govern themselves as a democracy. While it commonly has been assumed that press freedom carried a responsibility to be accurate, fair, and thorough, this responsibility was not stipulated in the First Amendment. It has evolved as the press's role has evolved.

Journalism, as an institution, has undergone many broad changes in the United States since the first journals of the colonial period, but the greatest transformation has taken place in the twentieth century. Major factors in the transformation include the following:

1. Improvements in technology, particularly since World War II. Advances in high-speed transmission and reproduction have led to a vast expansion of the means for collecting and dispensing information.

2. Broadening of interests. Because of improved communications, more information has become knowable at a time when living has become more complex and disorderly. This has created demand for more information about more subjects.

3. Rise of broadcasting. Radio and television have introduced instantaneous reporting and audiovisual emphasis, forcing the print media to seek alternative approaches to the news.

4. Changes in audience. People are better educated, more sophisticated about the new and different, younger on the whole, and increasingly more oriented to the electronic media than to the old-time newspaper.

5. Institutionalization of the media. The news system has become a giant industry with constant competition in the face of rising costs and the complexities of automation.

All these developments, absorbed into the historical framework of journalism, have affected the ways in which media people regard, gather, write, interpret, and present the news.

Although news reaches the public through many channels, the concepts, purposes, and responsibilities involved in the process are relatively constant among the media.

The styles of news presentation may vary, but the methods of selecting and gathering the news generally follow the pattern that has evolved in the newspaper system. For this reason, and because it still is the primary mass communicator of information and opinion, the newspaper is given widest attention in this book. Wherever possible, the statistics used are for 1975, to indicate the status of the news system at the start of the last quarter of the twentieth century.

There are signs that the system's status could change drastically in the future as the information/communications revolution proceeds. The increased use of computers, satellites, cable television, and other new technologies could force a redefinition of news.

Journalism and the Media provides a picture of where the news system has been and stands now, and a glimpse at where it is headed. The book is designed for use generally by anyone interested in journalism as a social force, and more specifically by the beginning journalist and the student aspiring to a career in mass communications.

NOTE

1. Henry Grunwald, "Don't Love the Press, But Understand It," *Time*, July 8, 1974, pp. 74–75.

1
The Role of Journalism and the Media

The function of journalism and the news media is to transmit information, to enlighten the public by reporting and explaining what is happening in the world. Journalists serve as the public's eyes and ears. The news media are the print and electronic means by which journalists relay what they see and hear. The media have a dual character: They are private businesses, but they perform a public service under constitutional protection against government interference. Aside from dispensing information, the principal functions of the media are influence, advertising, and entertainment. A traditional aspect of the media's role is an adversary posture—as a public watchdog keeping a check on government and other institutions.

THE "DESIRE" AND "RIGHT" TO KNOW

The "desire to know," to obtain information, is inherent in human nature. People are instinctively curious. They have a primal urge to communicate, to exchange ideas and attitudes, to learn the "news," to seek the truth. It is such interaction that makes a society function with some semblance of order.

The "right to know"—the right of an individual to know about matters that concern or interest him—is one of the enduring principles of United States society. This right, sometimes expressed as a "need to know," is implicit in the concept of a democratic community based on the will of the people. An individual must have information about his community, and the world beyond his community, if he is to make intelligent judgments about the direction of his life and the conduct of his government. He must have knowledge of events so that he can prepare to deal with them.

It is this right to know, for example, that compels disclosure of information about a proposed public school so that citizens can decide whether or not they want to vote for a budget that provides for its construction. It is this right that induces members of Congress, as representatives of the people, to hold hearings on a political scandal.

An individual is limited in his capability for gathering information beyond his immediate experience. He cannot be in two places at once. He cannot see across oceans, or even across town. He does not have sufficient time or resources to check with everyone who might have information about his concerns and interests. In short, he needs help for his eyes and ears.

Responsibility of Journalists. Acting as eyes and ears for the public is the function of journalists and their media. Clifton Daniel, when he was managing editor of the *New York Times*, said: "The duty of the reporter and editor, in Walter Lippmann's words, is to do 'what every sovereign citizen is supposed to do, but has not the time or interest to do for himself'—that is, to gather information, pick out what is important, digest it thoroughly, and without passion or prejudice relate it to the problems of the day."[1]

That duty long ago earned the press the name "Fourth Estate." Thomas Carlyle is credited ₁with the observation: "[Edmund] Burke said there were three estates in Parliament, but in the Reporters' Gallery yonder, there sat a Fourth Estate, more important [by] far than them all." A more modern version for the American press is "the fourth branch of government."

News in the broadest sense has always been a part of the human situation, but the task of gathering and reporting the news has grown increasingly complex as societies have become more complex. Billions of events and conflicts and happenings occur continually in the modern world of 4 billion people. Covering them all is an impossible mission; it is the role of the news system to try to select and cover the most significant and interesting.

Every day thousands of scattered journalists, acting as the public's proxies, observe countless happenings and report information about them via a communications network that reaches into every community. Newspapers and radio and television newscasts provide information not only about a local school board meeting and a congressional hearing in Washington, but also about the latest developments in an Asian war, the victims of a highway accident in a nearby town, the gossip in Hollywood, and the scores of last night's baseball games in a dozen cities. Newspapers also offer information about the price of milk at the neighborhood supermarket and the programs on TV tonight.

The Barrage of Information. Americans are swamped by information in various forms, more than the average household can absorb. An immense number of signals compete for attention. As of 1975, there were 1,756 daily newspapers with a combined circulation of 60,655,431 and a readership of at least double that figure (plus 8,824 weekly and semiweekly papers, with a typical individual circulation of about 2,000). Television sets were in 97 percent of all homes, and radio sets in 98.6 percent (not to mention car radios and pocket transistors). At least 8,000 magazines, both general and specialized, flooded the mails and newsstands. And interrelated with these media were the press associations (the backbone of the news system) and syndicates, and the vast network of advertising agencies and public relations firms whose business it is to feed information to the media.

The Habit of News. The United States now is so media-oriented that most people could not imagine life without the daily newspaper and the evening newscast. Following the news has become a habit, a daily ritual, regardless of the content. Whether this is good or bad depends on the viewpoint.

Author Mark Harris, jabbing at news addiction with a paraphrase of Lenin, wrote in 1974 that "the media are the opiate of the people." He added, "We have permitted the world of the journalist to become more real to us than the world of our senses, thus restricting our options and suffocating our imaginations."[2]

Whether one takes Harris serious or not, and whether most Americans stop to think about it or not, there is no denying that the media play a vital role in influencing individual thinking and shaping the values and culture of society. Ben H. Bagdikian, in his book *The Information Machines*, suggests the nature of this role:

> News is the peripheral nervous system of the body politic, sensing the total environment and selecting which sights and sounds shall be transmitted to the public. More than any other single mechanism, it decides which of the countless billions of events in the world shall be known to the generality of men. Having done so, it alters men's perceptions of the world and of themselves; the more rapid and vivid the communications, the greater is this alteration.[3]

THE PRINCIPLE OF A FREE PRESS

While other functions have grown in emphasis over the years, the supplying of information, or news in its broadest sense, has been regarded as the foremost role of the press since the United States was formed in 1789. The Founding Fathers, though they sometimes used the press to promote their own political interests, recognized the principle championed by Thomas Jefferson and other respected thinkers of the time—that a republic, if it is to work properly, must have a free flow of facts and ideas among the people.

A Protected Public Service. The principle of free exchange of information reflected the strong desire of America's leaders to escape the censorship and regulation that English rulers imposed on information and ideas they did not like. Before United States independence, control over the colonial press was exerted by British authorities, and the government's heavy-handed attitude curtailed the growth of newspapers. The Founding Fathers realized that knowledge is power, and they assumed that a free press would provide a check on the government—and against tyranny.

Perhaps the strongest statement in support of this concept was made by James Madison: "Knowledge will forever govern ignorance. And a people who mean to be their own governors must arm themselves with the power knowledge gives. A popular government without popular information or the means of acquiring it, is but a prologue to a farce, or a tragedy, or perhaps both."

To assure freedom of expression, the Founding Fathers included a specific protection of the press, along with other basic human rights, in the First Amendment to the Constitution: "Congress shall make no law respecting an establishment of religion, or prohibiting the free exercise thereof; *or abridging the freedom of speech, or of the press*;* or the right of people peaceably to assemble, and to petition the Government for a redress of grievances."

The theory was that a free and independent press would keep the people informed not only about the current life but also about the actions—and inactions—of the government; and at the same time it would keep public officials informed about opinions of the people. Since the public officials would be inclined to put their best foot forward, the government would not be the sole source of information about the government; rather, the press would be free to investigate and monitor the government in the public's interest, if necessary to act as an adversary. Anyone who wished could publish printed matter, immune from prior restraint or any other control by Presidents or the Congress and similar authorities at lower levels.

Thus, an independent press was seen as a public service. By providing a free flow of information and ideas—good and bad, and representing all viewpoints—it would be the means of securing higher values, notably individual rights and viable popular government. The First Amendment protection was intended as a benefit not for the press proprietors, but for the people in general.

An Independent Commercial Enterprise. If the news agencies were to be out of the hands of government, this meant that the important responsibility of gathering and disseminating information was to be entrusted to private, independent individuals and the "news" businesses they could establish and maintain. If there was to be no financial support from the government, it

* Italics supplied.

followed that, in order to operate—indeed, to survive in the competitive marketplace—the news businesses had to make money.

That the press was established under control of commercial interests in a democratic context had implications for the future that the Founding Fathers could not possibly foresee. It meant that the press, as a profitmaking business, would be a part of the economic system and, as the country became industrialized, would become oriented to marketing in its relationship to the social order.

At various times segments of the media have had subsidy support from the government, labor and industry, religious denominations, philanthropic foundations, and special-interest groups; but the basic support pattern that emerged for the principal news media was almost total reliance on revenues from advertising and sales of the news product. This pattern inevitably placed a heavy premium on appeal to the widest possible audience, which, in turn, was an important determinant in the selection of information offered by the media.

Throughout American history, anyone with the desire and money to publish a newspaper has been able to do so virtually without government interference, so long as there was conformance with the laws of libel, obscenity, privacy, and contempt of court. The same has been true for magazines, books, and films (this does not mean, however, that any of the media has been protected from other forms of restrictive pressures, such as political, social, or religious).

Radio and television, which did not come until the twentieth century, have somewhat different rules than those for the print media. Ownership and operation of a station is subject to license by the Federal Communications Commission (FCC), which regulates station distribution and sets certain operating standards. The reason for the regulation is to prevent monopoly control of the airwaves, which are considered to be in the public domain and are limited in number.

A Libertarian Concept. The initial concept of the American press was based on the seventeenth- and eighteenth-century libertarian philosophy shaped by such theorists as John Milton, Isaac Newton, John Locke, and Adam Smith. This philosophy saw people as naturally rational, free, equal, and moral, all seeking knowledge and truth in the "marketplace of ideas." The emphasis was on individual fulfillment through knowledge; it was believed that as each individual pursued his own enlightened self-interest, society would benefit.

Finding the truth required free interplay of information and ideas which, in turn, required a free press as an aid to communication. Under the libertarian theory, there was no constraint to be nonpartisan. Truth would emerge because rational people, when presented all the options, would be able to distinguish truth from falsehood; and being also moral, they would act correctly on the basis of the truth.

Two factors bore significantly on the press concept as formulated by the Founding Fathers:

First, the constitutional protection granted "negative" freedom. The First Amendment said Congress could "pass no law" abridging the freedom, but it did not define what the freedom was. The Amendment did not stipulate that the press's freedom carried the responsibility to be truthful or fair or even intelligent. It was left up to the press proprietors and the public to decide exactly what constituted press freedom and how it was to be used.

Second, the notion of the "governing people" in late-eighteenth-century America was very narrow. At that time, the population was 4 million, mostly agrarian, dispersed, and uneducated. Few could read or write—or vote. By law, all women, men who did not own property and could not read or write, slaves, and indentured servants were excluded from voting and otherwise participating in government. In effect, it was the educated elite —including landowners, merchants, politicians, and most of the publishers—who were directly involved in the "marketplace of ideas" and government.

With the passing of time, the libertarian aspect of the press concept became obscured. New social, economic, and intellectual factors came into play. These included political and industrial competition, universal education, and suffrage. Questions were raised about man's basic nature as conceived in the libertarian thinking. Emerging public criticism took two broad directions: first, that the performance of segments of the press, within the changing environment, was too narrow and partisan and was not leading to the desired result—the good of society as a whole; and second, that as the media became larger and more powerful, access to these channels of expression became restricted.

The libertarian heritage continued to influence the general conception of the press, but gradually there developed a concept of public accountability to fill the responsibility gap in the First Amendment. The emphasis shifted from the individual to society as a whole, and the press was seen as a common carrier—much like the public utilities and the railroads but without their government regulation.

This new concept was a featured point of the 1947 report of the Commission on Freedom of the Press (called the Hutchins Commission after its chairman, Robert M. Hutchins). The concept also is reflected in today's ethical and professional standards of journalism, although debate continues about how closely the standards are followed by some of the press.

BASIC FUNCTIONS OF THE NEWS MEDIA

Though the American media have taken many twists and turns during their 200-year evolution, four functions have emerged as principal in the system's operations: information, influence, advertising, and entertainment. The degree of emphasis given to each function depends on the medium, and the effects of any function often overlap those of others.

Information. Within the broad context of this function, the media enlighten the public about what is happening in the world. They also service the political system by informing the people about the business of their governments, and they protect personal liberties by monitoring legislation and law enforcement.

The first American newspapers, generally founded in seaports, had very limited access to information. They obtained their news from British newspapers or from travelers and anyone else who happened to pass the door. The information was not necessarily current, correct, or complete. The emphasis was on politics and public affairs, usually from slanted views, and on trading and shipping. As transportation and printing improved and readership increased, the papers added news about such topics as crime, literature, industry, and the activities of average people. Today all these topics—and much more of public concern and interest—are covered by the media.

In a news sense, the newspapers and newsmagazines are the primary purveyors of information. General magazines, and to a greater degree the trade magazines, provide information about fewer subjects in each issue, but usually more information about each subject. Radio and television are basically entertainment media and, compared with newspapers, contribute little to the popular enlightenment.

Influence. This function also enlightens, with the purpose of persuading the public to a certain viewpoint. The process includes presentation of a variety of ideas and viewpoints, media leadership in public affairs, and public-service reporting to improve the community.

Efforts to influence public opinion have always been a part of American journalism. Early newspapers paid more attention to views than to news. They printed opinion openly and twisted news of events so as to promote a certain viewpoint or cause. In the mid-nineteenth century, editorial pages began to appear, and they have been a staple of newspapers ever since.

Today the average newspaper and many magazines include not only textual editorials representing the views of the publication's owners but also editorial cartoons, columns reflecting the opinions of individual journalists, letters to the editor from readers, and commentaries or analyses of current events and issues. Many papers in recent years have added an "op-ed" (opposite the editorial page) page in an effort to provide a greater variety of views, particularly those that differ from the paper's own opinions. Contributions to the op-ed page—on almost any subject—are printed from ordinary people as well as public figures.

An increasing number of radio stations, particularly the all-news stations, are broadcasting editorials, usually about local issues. A few television stations have followed suit. Many broadcast documentaries tend to stress a viewpoint and thus, indirectly at least, are a form of persuasion.

Advertising. By bringing together buyers and sellers of goods and services, this function services the nation's economic system.

Its purpose is to market merchandise—at a price to advertisers.

In the early newspapers advertisements were few and took the form of political and shipping notices. But as free education produced more readers, improved printing and transmission processes produced more papers to circulate, and more industries produced more goods to sell, the economic benefits of expanded advertising were realized. Increased advertising revenue for the newspapers not only meant the end of political subsidies, but also meant profits for the newspaper owners. And since newspapers were conceived as commercial enterprises, profits were a primary concern of the owners. Thus advertising was looked upon as a necessary ingredient of both the public-service and business aspects of the press.

The greatest impetus for advertising came from the Industrial Revolution, which resulted in a system of mass production of consumer goods that needed mass markets. In order for the economy to keep going, the goods had to be sold; for the goods to be sold, information about them had to reach potential consumers; and for information to flow to the consumers, the logical channel was the media.

Eventually advertising became an integral part of the national economic process, and an accepted function of the media. Today advertising is the economic foundation of newspapers, magazines, and broadcasting. Many newspaper readers, in fact, look to the ads as a service as much as the news.

The average newspaper fills about two-thirds of its space with advertisements—display and classified—and derives approximately 80 percent of its income from advertising. Broadcast stations fill the air with from two to ten or twelve commercial messages an hour, and most obtain all of their income from advertising.

Entertainment. This is the primary function of most radio and television. It gets strong stress in general magazines and many specialized magazines that deal with such subjects as recreation and humor. It is occupying more and more space in newspapers—perhaps half in some.

One purpose of the entertainment function is simply to amuse a reader, listener, or viewer, to divert him and give him emotional release from his daily cares. This is not an altogether altruistic motivation, and it is linked to a second purpose: Entertainment has wide appeal, and attracts customers; it therefore is an economic factor. The larger the audience, the greater is the medium's potential for marketing merchandise and collecting advertising revenue. For the print media, larger audiences also mean more sales income.

A third purpose of entertainment, some social scientists believe, is persuasion. Research has shown that newspaper features, magazine articles, or TV programs that are diverting can at the same time be a subtle form of influence on people's thinking. Political cartoons and many comics, for instance, carry messages.

The entertainment function is generally regarded as divided into two broad categories: one is entertaining news, and the other is features about self-help, leisure activities, sports, culture, and entertainment itself.

Entertaining news emphasizes human interest written with a light touch. It deals with events involving oddity, humor, conflict, excitement, pathos, sex; but the events in themselves are not necessarily significant. Newspapers and magazines have included entertaining news since the days of the penny press in the 1830s.

Features about leisure activities have increased in recent years as people have acquired more leisure time. All the media have added or expanded "lifestyle" sections, and there is an endless stream of "how-to" information about bridge, photography, horoscopes, travel, recreation, gardening, home repairs, cooking, personal problems. Similarly, there is increasing emphasis on art, music, drama, literature. Sports and comics are among the most popular media offerings.

Varying Emphasis. The prevalence of the four functions varies with the medium and, in the case of newspapers, has changed with time.

Of the four functions, there never has been any doubt that advertising and entertainment have had first call in broadcasting. News, or information, is largely a by-product which is given comparatively little air time. Editorial opinion amounts to a smattering.

In newspapers, live, or "hard," news still occupies the front page, but it has been giving way to advertising and entertainment on the inside pages. Publishers argue, despite continuing high profits, that increased advertising is needed to pay for rising operational costs; and entertainment draws the readers sought by the advertisers.

Marketing studies of readers' preferences in recent years have pointed to more consumer reporting, how-to-cope articles, and lifestyle and leisure-time features, usually at the expense of national and world news. In a study of 25 newspapers (weighted toward the larger papers because they cover most daily readership in the country), Ben H. Bagdikian found that the average paper got much fatter between 1950 and 1970, but that 83 percent of the added pages went to advertising.[4] The space for news also expanded, but an increasing share of that space was devoted to "soft" news such as real estate, food and fashions, sports and business, and "special" sections unrelated to live news.

At the same time, opinion and interpretation have crept up, with the addition of more viewpoint columns, letters to the editor, and news analyses to supplement the editorials. Bagdikian's study showed that many editorial pages had grown in the 20 years from fractions of a page to full pages. Still, the space devoted to opinion is slight compared to advertising and entertainment.

THE DUAL-ROLE DEBATE

The twin character of the news media as private business and public service raises the question of whether there is a built-in conflict of interest between the need to make profits and the responsibility to present the news fairly, accurately, intelligently, and thoroughly. A. J. Liebling, one of the first professional commentators on the press, wrote: "The function of the press in society is to inform, but its role is to make money."[5]

Many critics argue that the heavy reliance on advertising invites loss of independence, through pressures from advertisers and the diminution of print space or air time that could be devoted to news. They say that a strong emphasis on entertainment to attract larger audiences (and thus more revenue from sales and advertising) dilutes the media's fare and detracts from news about serious and significant events of public concern.

The counterargument, granted the accepted nature of the

media as private enterprises, is that the financial health of a news company and its ability to perform public services are interdependent. A familiar maxim among media executives is that good journalism is both good public service and good business.

In this view, a company that does a good job of reporting and interpreting the news is performing a respected service that appeals to a large audience and thus attracts advertising that ensures financial stability. Conversely, the firmer the fiscal security the greater is the company's capability for turning out a quality product; and the greater is its independence to resist outside pressures, including those from an advertiser.

In the final analysis, the news media are accountable not only to their owners and stockholders but also to the professional traditions and standards of competitive journalism—and to the public. A news organization that fails to uphold these standards and retain the respect and trust of the public is likely to lose its customers and advertisers—and hence, die.

THE PRESS AND GOVERNMENT

A pivotal part of the press's information function is its relationship with government. Within its public-service context, the press services the government by relaying information necessary for the orderly functioning of society; at the same time the press checks on the government against secrecy, deceit, misdeeds, and oppression. Ideally, the two services are performed in some semblance of balance, but performance has been inconsistent. As William L. Rivers says in his book *The Adversaries,* "At times in our history, government and press have been the most savage adversaries, and at other times they have been such sweethearts that much of the press has been incorporated into the machinery of power."[6]

Servicing the Government. Because the master plan for the United States deliberately omitted an official information system within the government, the free press has had to serve as a transmission belt for government information needed by the people to be good citizens of a democracy. Such information covers the whole spectrum of governmental concerns—from waging war, negotiating foreign agreements, and legislating new laws to taxation, court rulings, and trade regulations. This transmission is continuous and extends down to the local school board and sewer commission.

The media also service officialdom in another way: most officials read newspapers and listen to newscasts regularly as a check on events, public opinion, and political climate.

The importance of the transmission process and the voluminous amount of government information that must be disseminated have led to a giant, expensive information and public relations bureaucracy within the federal government, from the White House down. Every federal department and agency, every congressional committee and military service, has an information office or employee whose primary responsibility is dealing with the press and releasing information for the taxpayers. The same kind of information structure exists at state, county, and municipal levels, its size and complexity commensurate with the size and needs of the government.

The information officials are generally the first line of contact that journalists have with government activities. For the most part the system works to everyone's mutual benefit: government offices get their information disseminated and reporters get the news they need for their stories.

Monitoring the Government. The information system is satisfactory as long as the government is open, honest, fair, and straightforward in dispensing its information. However, this is not always the case, although the United States government generally has been more open to the press than have the governments of most other countries. Many public officials are inclined toward secrecy, and it is the nature of most to try to "manage" the news in their administration's best interests. For this reason, the service aspect of the press's role has always been balanced with an adversary aspect—that is, a constant and skeptical vigilance over the government's actions, and inactions.

SECRECY. Most public officials emphasize their triumphs and minimize their defeats because their reputations and careers depend on favorable public opinion. Some may not have anything to hide, but they believe they can do a better job of running the government without kibitzing from the press and the public. And there are certain situations, such as diplomatic negotiations, military movements, and police pursuit of fugitives, in which it traditionally has been accepted that less than full disclosure can be in the national or public interest.

Whatever the reason, there seems to be a built-in institutional inclination toward what Russell Baker, the *New York Times* satirical columnist, called a "passion for secrets" that is antithetical to public participation in government. William L. Rivers, Theodore Peterson, and Jay W. Jensen concluded in their book *The Mass Media and Modern Society*: "In theory, America's leaders have wanted a free and independent press as a check upon government; in practice, they have wanted no such thing."[7]

Secrecy in the federal government began with the closed Constitutional Convention in 1787 and the first administration under George Washington. It has fluctuated in degree over the years, depending on world conditions and the administration in office. President Johnson, for instance, sometimes reversed decisions if they were disclosed before he wanted them made public. The Watergate investigations exposed the fact that President Nixon, angered at publication of his secrets, had formed a "plumbers unit" to try to stop the "leaks."

Since the Cold War days of nuclear confrontation and fears of Communism, the federal government has used the "national security" shield to withhold information—sometimes justifiably, sometimes not. In recent years the secrecy stamp has been lifted at least from routine federal records as the result of the Freedom of Information Act.

Sessions of both houses of Congress have been open to the public since 1795, but many congressional committee meetings have remained closed. The same is true of many executive departmental meetings. And the tendency toward secrecy is perhaps even greater at lower levels of government, where decisions are made that more directly affect the people's daily living. Police and courts, for example, frequently refuse to divulge information about arrests and trials, despite the possibility of violation of constitutional due process.

NEWS MANAGEMENT. The other side of the coin is that public officials must have popular support to remain and function in office, and usually are eager to release information if it suits that end. Historically, public servants have tried to "manage" the news so that their own views and strong points are widely publicized. This practice has been exemplified most visibly by Presidents, because of their unique position and authority, but it has existed down the line into the village hall.

There are many strategies for trying to manage the news, all directed at winning sympathetic treatment from reporters. In recent times, Presidents and other officials have bypassed reporters to reach the public directly via television. While these strategies do not necessarily imply evil intentions, they are aimed at influencing public opinion.

President Theodore Roosevelt, a flamboyant master of press agentry, met informally with reporters of his choosing, knowing they were sympathetic to spreading his views. Franklin D. Roosevelt had a knack for manipulating press conferences and held many; when he felt it was advisable to go directly to the public, he scheduled a "fireside chat" on radio, a technique he introduced. Harry S. Truman earned a generally good press with his informality and plain talk. Dwight D. Eisenhower relied on the public relations skills of his press secretary, James Hagerty, to retain his "war hero" image.

John F. Kennedy, handsome and articulate, created an enduring "Camelot" aura despite some notable setbacks during his administration. He opened up the White House to correspondents, granted exclusive interviews to favorite reporters, permitted live coverage of his televised news conferences, and mingled socially with many journalists.

By contrast, Lyndon B. Johnson preferred face-to-face contact in small informal meetings which he could control with his domineering personality. In an attempt to stay favorably in the news, he kept up a steady flow of speeches, messages to Congress, publicized trips, and "leaks" to favored correspondents. In the main he was successful until his administration became engulfed in the Vietnam War and his attempts at news management created a "credibility gap."

Richard M. Nixon, never friendly with the press, preferred techniques that avoided direct questioning by correspondents. He concentrated on "packaged" public relations and on nationally televised statements. His final falling-out with the press began when TV commentators followed his statements with analytical reactions and criticism. Then, in an effort to retain public support, Nixon sought to discredit his press critics—

as with Vice President Spiro Agnew's attacks on the "liberal" media and the "Eastern Establishment."

Jimmy Carter had many presidential lessons to draw from. He saw the impact of television and exploited it as soon as he entered the White House (an article about Carter in the *New York Times Magazine* was headlined "The Prime-Time President"). Projecting a "cool" and folksy image, he early attracted wide attention with his walk down Pennsylvania Avenue on Inauguration Day, a town meeting in Massachusetts, an informal fireside chat, telephone call-ins from people around the country—all naturals for sympathetic press coverage and public appeal.

PRESS SUSCEPTIBILITY. That reporters sometimes may be susceptible to news-management strategies can perhaps be attributed to several factors.

One is the feeling of flattery that comes with sharing information about the workings of government, of "being in on the action." Another is the sense of authority attached to information dispensed by officials involved in the action, who deal daily with the complexities of budgets, law enforcement, or military movements ("the Defense Secretary has classified information that we don't have").

Then, too, a reporter is subject to a system of rewards and punishments from valuable news sources, which can be crucial to his performance on a competitive news beat. A friendly "leak" is welcome, but hostile silence on an important matter can kill a story. A reporter constantly faces deadlines and other pressures to get the latest and most interesting news into print or on the air. Finally, there is the possibility—that no good journalist would admit—that laziness and complacency of some reporters allow government handouts to be accepted at face value.

DECEPTION. Whether or not the press historically has been too ready to rely on the statement by the official source, as some critics have contended, the danger in secrecy and "managed" news is obvious: Public opinion can be misled into distorted impressions of how things are. Sometimes the consequences are disastrous. When this happens, the people's confidence in their government is undermined. A few classic examples of government deception at the federal level illustrate the point.

In 1960 when Francis Gary Powers's U-2 spy plane went down over the Soviet Union, the Eisenhower administration, through the Central Intelligence Agency, issued a cover story that the missing craft had been a weather plane that had wandered off course from a Turkish base. Six days later the Russians announced that the plane was found on Soviet territory and presented documented proof that it had been spying. The United States was forced to admit its deceit.

During the Vietnam War, the Kennedy and Johnson administrations repeatedly told the country that the war was going well for the South Vietnamese and the United States when it was in fact going poorly. As documented in David Halberstam's book *The Best and the Brightest*, correspondents in Vietnam encountered difficulties covering the war firsthand. They were forced to use military transportation to get around the country and had to depend for much of their information on government briefings in Saigon. When a few correspondents managed to get into the war zones and sent back pessimistic reports, the government tried to discredit them and have them withdrawn. The Vietnam shadow eventually darkened everything else in the Johnson administration, and the widening "credibility gap" was a major factor in the President's decision not to seek reelection in 1968.

The Vietnam deception continued under the Nixon administration (for example, the secret bombing of Cambodia), and the President and his "palace guard" retreated behind the wall of secrecy they built around the White House. Their Vietnam ventures were soon eclipsed by the Watergate scandal, which exposed malefactions in domestic matters as well. The subsequent lying, cover-ups, and criminal actions led to Nixon's forced resignation, and to still greater public distrust of government.

An example of a more subtle type of news management was the "war on poverty" launched by the Johnson administration. It illustrated how manipulation of information, however well intentioned, can mislead an accommodating press—and thus the public. The government publicized plans for various programs for the disadvantaged, with obvious political profit; and the press disseminated the publicity with little questioning. The publicity raised expectations, but eventually the fanfare died out and for the most part the programs never materialized.

THIRD FORCE. Occasionally the media are forced into an adversary posture by default because of a void in the governmental power alignment. In this sense the media have been seen as a third political force acting as guardian of the two-party system. This has been particularly true in recent decades when the authority of the presidency has grown at the expense of Congress. For example, David S. Broder, political writer for the *Washington Post*, wrote of the press's part in exposing the Watergate scandal: "The silence Democratic leaders have adopted in their quest for nonpartisanship has left it to the press to provide the commentary and, on occasion, the rebuttal, to the vigorous efforts by Mr. Nixon and his allies to shape public opinion to his own ends."[8]

Broder and other commentators felt the situation was similar during the Vietnam War, on the ground that the Republicans failed to question adequately the war policies of the Kennedy and Johnson administrations.

WITHHELD NEWS. On occasion the media have withheld news "for security reasons," sometimes at the request of the government. The *New York Times*, for instance, knew about the U-2 flights long before Powers went down, but did not print the fact until the Russians found Powers's plane. The *Times* knew of plans for the disastrous, illegal invasion of Cuba at the Bay of Pigs in 1961, but, at President Kennedy's request, did not publish a story (although other papers wrote about preparations). After the invasion failed, Kennedy told the *Times*'s managing editor, Turner Catledge, that in retrospect he wished the press had printed more information, on the ground that public opinion might have been aroused, forcing cancellation of the invasion.

By the 1970s, after Vietnam and Watergate, most newspapers were reluctant to withhold information, except in cases where lives might be jeopardized. From experience, editors tended to feel that government officials were not always the best judges of what was necessary for national security, or "in the public's interest."

Over objections from the Nixon administration, the *New*

York Times, remembering the Bay of Pigs lesson, published the Pentagon Papers about the conduct of the Vietnam War; later, A. M. Rosenthal, executive editor of the *Times*, was quoted as saying that "no great disaster befell the American people from the publication." The *Washington Post* broke a story about the Central Intelligence Agency's secret payments to Jordan's King Hussein, and, in the face of charges of "irresponsible journalism," defended the action as being in the public's interest.

Such episodes always stir controversy over the question of secrecy in the name of national security versus the press's privilege to publish in the name of the people's right to know. Following the Hussein disclosure, Thomas Griffith of *Time* magazine put the issue in some perspective in his "Newswatch" column:

> The courts have long upheld the rights of editors to decide for themselves. This privilege is not as cost-free as some editors argue: Foreign political leaders often deplore and consider harmful the sievelike nature of the American Government and the blabbiness of the American press. The gain is a public informed, in time to redress wrongs. Advantage and disadvantage are not always in neat balance. Where in other societies only authority prevails, here what is not authority's domain is left to conscience. The heartening fact, to judge by the record, is that the graver the issue, the more the editor hears from his conscience.[9]

THE PRESS AND POLITICS

The media, serving as a conduit, have always played a major role in politics and elections; but the role has been magnified by television and by continuing changes in the political process. In the old days candidates were chosen primarily in smoky back rooms by political power brokers and heavy campaign contributors, and the press recorded the process and the results. Today, the selection of candidates is more open among political convention delegates or through primary elections, and aspirants rely heavily on media exposure that includes public-relations "packaging" and TV commercials.

Having learned the "image" lesson of the 1960 Kennedy-Nixon TV debates, candidates now consider the public-relations or TV expert an indispensable member of their staffs. Position papers, which tend to be dull and attract little media attention, have given way to staged "media events," for example, at housing developments and picketed factories. The emphasis has swung away from substance to style.

Here again is the possibility of "news management." It takes a sophisticated and politically wise journalist to see through politicians' efforts to manipulate the cameras and coverage. At the same time, the journalist has unprecedented opportunities to enlighten the public about the candidates and issues through astute analyses and interpretations. Whatever the case, its expanded role has given the press new responsibilities in the political process.

THE PRESS AND OTHER INSTITUTIONS

What is true of the press in relation to government is also true in its relation to other institutions and special-interest groups. The press acts as intermediary, transmitting information about business, education, scientific development, culture—and also providing public feedback. The objective is understanding between the institutions and their publics in the interest of an open and a smooth-functioning society.

As with government, conditions exist for secrecy and news management by these other institutions. Businesses, universities, school systems, scientific "think tanks," and museums have public-relations officials whose inclination is to emphasize good points and minimize bad ones. Thus, as surrogate for the public, the press plays the adversary, monitoring for fraud, mismanagement, and misuse of public funds.

It would be misleading to say that only the "establishment" institutions and groups need monitoring and are capable of managing the news; many special-interest groups and anti-establishment activists, with little official power in the normal sense, have also learned the techniques for attracting attention and manipulating news coverage. Two obvious examples were the civil-rights marchers and the anti–Vietnam War demonstrators. Both groups recognized the power of television cameras for getting their views known and soliciting sympathy.

THE URGE TO INVESTIGATE

The adversary role puts a premium on investigative reporting. In the broadest sense, all reporting involves investigation. There have been special investigations of social ills since the crusading of James Gordon Bennett, Horace Greeley, and Joseph Pulitzer in the nineteenth century and the magazine muckrakers of the early twentieth century. Newspapers, large and small, have regularly flushed out crime and political chicanery and have delved into every conceivable situation, from prison conditions to industrial pollution to mistreatment in mental health programs.

New Emphasis. In the 1970s, in the wake of Vietnam and Watergate, the media put new emphasis on in-depth investigations, as described in *The New Muckrakers* by Leonard Downie, Jr.[10] *Life* set the pattern with an investigative team in the magazine's dying days of the late 1960s, a pattern that was followed by a string of reporters who acquired a sort of folk-hero status with their aggressive probes. Among them were Bob Woodward and Carl Bernstein of the *Washington Post*, who gained fame with their Watergate stories; Washington columnist Jack Anderson; Seymour Hersh of the *New York Times*; Jack Nelson of the *Los Angeles Times*; Robert Greene of *Newsday*; Donald Barlett and James Steele of the *Philadelphia Inquirer*; I. F. Stone, who suddenly found new public recognition for the investigating he had been doing all along with his weekly newsletter.

Many large newspapers and the wire services turned loose teams of reporters to investigate situations both in government and in other institutions. The teams commonly worked for months—poring over records, traveling extensively, and interviewing scores of people—to gather information for long exposés or explanatory articles. The investigations sought not only to chronicle the effects of events but also to interpret the causes.

Press investigations, for example, turned the spotlight on the long-shielded Central Intelligence Agency and the Federal Bureau of Investigation. The probes uncovered activities, such as illegal wiretapping, that the public had never known about.

In a notable exposure of corporate misdeeds, the *Wall Street Journal* initiated an investigation, later joined by other newspapers, that uncovered corporate payoffs, political contributions, and bribes aimed at winning business favors from officials of foreign countries. The investigation led to political shake-ups in several countries, the firing of top officials from some of the world's largest corporations, and the development of corporate codes and reforms to prevent such activities in the future. The *Journal* said its two-year campaign alone accounted for 480 news stories in its pages.

Broadcasting's Minor Role. Although many people get their news primarily from television, the broadcast media have done little investigative reporting. They have produced some worthy documentaries in the early Edward R. Murrow's and Fred W. Friendly's *See It Now* tradition of the Columbia Broadcasting System, but they have been few. At the network level, they have included studies of the Pentagon, health care, hunger, and pensions. At the local level, stations have looked into such subjects as pollution, nuclear power safety, slum housing, rising prices, consumer fraud, crime, and prison and hospital conditions. In the mid-1970s only the CBS program *60 Minutes* concentrated on investigation on a sustaining basis. Otherwise, the broadcast media largely reported the results of investigations by the print media.

The nature of the broadcast media tends to militate against in-depth investigation. Radio and television are subject to some government regulation, which could inhibit probes into government activities. The broadcast media obtain virtually all their revenues from advertisers, who resist programs critical of business and industry. The production of documentaries costs hundreds of thousands of dollars, and the resultant programs usually run a deficit because they draw small audiences and thus are not attractive to advertisers. Local stations are handicapped because they do not have the manpower for long investigations.

In a sense, however, the broadcast media have acted as a catalyst for newspaper investigative work. Because the broadcast media generally are first in reporting "live" events, newspapers have sought new approaches to news about the events. Among

the approaches are expanded information and in-depth interpretation and analysis—all of which involve investigative reporting.

THE ADVOCATES AND "NEW" JOURNALISTS

The unrest and upheavals of the 1960s provoked some
journalists to break out of the traditional mold. These journalists sought alternative ways, both in content and style, to try to
change society, particularly the "Establishment."

Advocacy Journalism. Sometimes called "point of view" journalism, this approach developed mainly in "alternative" and
underground newspapers and magazines. It was activist, subjective, reformist. It made no pretense of separating editorial
comment from objective reporting. The reporters and editors
injected their own views into the stories. This philosophy was
perhaps typified by a widely circulated comment by Bruce
Brugman, editor/publisher of the *San Francisco Bay Guardian*
(which adopted the credo "It is the newspaper's duty to print the
news and raise hell"): "I feel we must do more than print the
news, since disclosure itself may not be enough to bring change."

Advocacy journalism reflected the general frustration of the
era and complaints that the conservative Establishment and the
conventional press were not paying enough attention to youth,
women, minority groups, the poor, and the downtrodden.
Among the pioneers in this category were the *Village Voice* in
New York, the *Phoenix* in Boston, and the *Bay Guardian* and
Rolling Stone in San Francisco.

New Journalism. Closely allied to advocacy was a style called
"new journalism," which was characterized by impressionistic
writing. "New Journalism" included subjective reports by parti-
cipants in events, and evaluations by experts with special knowledge or prestige. A leading spirit of this new form was Tom
Wolfe. Others were Norman Mailer, who wrote an impressionistic account of the Vietnam War protesters' march on the
Pentagon, and Jimmy Breslin, who graphically described the
Chicago riots during the 1968 Democratic political convention.

This new journalism usually was in long essay format and
purported to re-create the thoughts and feelings of the people
involved in the events. Some of the writing portrayed imaginary

characters as composites of real people. Critics of this form, while conceding it was entertaining, contended that it was more style than substance, and often more fiction than fact.

NOTES

1. Clifton Daniel, in a speech at the University of North Carolina, Oct. 21, 1960, reprinted in *The Responsibility of the Press*, ed. Gerald Gross (New York: Fleet Publishing Corporation, 1966), p. 150.
2. Mark Harris, "The Last Article," *New York Times Magazine*, Oct. 6, 1974, p. 20.
3. Ben H. Bagdikian, *The Information Machines* (New York: Harper Colophon Books, 1971), p. xii.
4. Bagdikian, "Fat Newspapers and Slim Coverage," *Columbia Journalism Review*, Sept./Oct. 1973, pp. 15–20.
5. A. J. Liebling, *The Press* (New York: Ballantine Books, 1964), p. 7.
6. William L. Rivers, *The Adversaries* (Boston: Beacon Press, 1970), p. 9.
7. William L. Rivers, Theodore Peterson, and Jay W. Jensen, *The Mass Media and Modern Society* (San Francisco: Rinehart Press, 1971), p. 105.
8. David S. Broder, quoted in "Press and Watergate: Intervening in History," *Columbia Journalism Review*, Sept./Oct. 1974, p. 7.
9. Thomas Griffith, "Editors Telling Secrets," *Time*, March 16, 1977, p. 80.
10. Leonard Downie, Jr., *The New Muckrakers* (Washington: New Republic Book Company, Inc., 1976).

SUGGESTED READING

Davison, Phillips W., Boylan, James, and Yu, Frederick T. C. *Mass Media*. New York: Praeger Publishers, 1976.

Gross, Gerald, ed. *The Responsibility of the Press*. New York: Fleet Publishing Corporation, 1966.

Lippmann, Walter. *Public Opinion*. New York: Macmillan, 1922.

Rivers, William L., Peterson, Theodore, and Jensen, Jay W. *The Mass Media and Modern Society*. San Francisco: Rinehart Press, 1971.

2

What Is News?

Every minute, every second, a myriad of events and happenings are taking place across the globe—births, deaths, accidents, natural calamities, fights, strikes, discoveries, meetings, announcements, sports contests, and so on into the endless mechanics of everyday living. Only a tiny fraction of all this is considered by journalists to be news. And only a fraction of the news actually gathered by any one newspaper or broadcast station gets into print or on the air. Whether or not an event or issue is newsworthy is determined by criteria that have evolved among journalists over the years.

DEFINITIONS OF NEWS

There have been many definitions of news, most of them familiar by now. One dictionary says news is "fresh information concerning something that has recently taken place." Another defines news as "tidings or intelligence of new or hitherto unknown things." A third: "Recent events and happenings, especially those that are unusual or notable."

Various editors have offered their own definitions. All generally recognize that news is intended to interest, inform, and, in some cases, entertain.

Joseph Pulitzer, the nineteenth-century editor and publisher of the *St. Louis Post-Dispatch* and the *New York World*, wanted news stories that were (as he put it) original, distinctive, dramatic, romantic, thrilling, unique, curious, quaint, humorous, odd, and apt to be talked about. Charles A. Dana, editor of the old *New York Sun*, felt that "anything that will make people talk" was news.

One of the most durable, though imprecise, definitions came from Turner Catledge, former managing editor of the *New York Times*, who called news "anything you can find out today that you didn't know before." And countless editors have merely told their staffs to find stories that would make the readers perk up and say, "Hey, I didn't know that!" All of which has led reporters to a favorite definition: "News is what my editor says it is."

News has been described as both a commodity and a state of mind. Journalism textbooks point out that news is gathered, processed, and packaged by profitmaking news organizations, like any other consumer product. At the same time it is something that stimulates interest in millions of people, often stirring them into action as a result. All news deals in some way with the traditional five W's and H—who, what, when, where, why, and how.

TYPES OF NEWS

Basically there are two kinds of spot, or "live," news: spontaneous and planned. Spontaneous news includes events such as a fire, an earthquake, an accident, a killing, an arrest. Planned news includes prearranged and anticipated events: that is, the news derives from a scheduled meeting, hearing, trial, press conference, speech, statement, demonstration, space launching, and the like. In a sense, a person or group or agency "makes" the planned news, which constitutes a large proportion of any day's news agenda.

A presidential press conference, for example, usually dominates the front pages and newscasts immediately afterward. President Carter's nationally televised press conference on July

28, 1977, a date chosen at random for illustration, resulted in the following coverage in a few selected morning newspapers:

New York Times. Page 1: Lead story—reaction to Israel's decision to legalize three Jewish settlements on the West Bank of the Jordan River. Delay in sale of radar planes to Iran. Reply to criticism of the White House's attitude toward the disadvantaged. Inside Pages: Announcement that nuclear test ban talks would begin. Transcript of the press conference. An analysis of the President's performance at the conference.

Washington Post. Page 1: West Bank settlements, disadvantaged, Iran. Inside Pages: Nuclear test talks and conference excerpts.

Milwaukee Journal. Page 1: *New York Times* analysis under heading "Interpreting the News." Inside Pages: Disadvantaged, Iran.

San Francisco Chronicle. Page 1: Iran, disadvantaged. Inside Pages: West Bank settlements, nuclear test talks.

VARIATIONS IN MEANING

No one definition of news is entirely satisfactory for every situation. Perhaps this is because the nature of news changes with the times, and the concept of what is newsworthy is subject to the judgments of both the editor and individuals within his audience.

Effects of Time. A half-century ago Charles A. Lindbergh's nonstop solo flight across the Atlantic Ocean was reported in banner headlines. It was a dramatic "first" in aviation, a conquest by man over nature. Measured against this "first," the second and subsequent transoceanic flights declined in newsworthiness. Today such flights by modern jets are common and do not rate public attention; they have been replaced in the news by flights to the moon and robot exploration of the planets.

Effects of Judgment. The way journalists look at the news is determined to a large extent by their company's policies, by what they consider to be their audience's principal interests, and by their own backgrounds and personal traits. Studies have shown, for example, that journalists are predominantly male, middle-class, and concentrated in large urban centers and disproportionately in the Northeast. These characteristics generally reflect those of the main body of the news media audience. It is no accident, then, that the media give wide attention to subjects of interest to men, such as sports, to established middle-class institutions, and to urban affairs.

On an individual basis, a journalist's news judgment is influenced by his own prejudices, suspicions, interests, and emotions. For example, an editor who feels that the condition of the environment is particularly important is inclined to emphasize this issue in his selection of news to present to the public.

Similarly, there are disparities among readers in how they view the significance or interest of different kinds of news. A plunge in the stock market may be of vital interest to a businessman, but a bore to a teenager. A woman may be fascinated by the latest Paris fashions; a man probably is not. A farmer wants to know about a new pest threat to crops; an industrial worker is more concerned about factory automation.

Examples of Differences. The effect of judgment factors on determining newsworthiness is illustrated by a study of American newspapers reported by *Los Angeles Times* media writer David Shaw.[1] In the study, the front pages of three of the country's leading newspapers—the *New York Times*, the *Washington Post*, and the *Los Angeles Times*—were examined every day during the first five months of 1977. According to Shaw, the study found vast differences among the three papers in judgment, interest, style, scope, and tone. For example:

- Only 28 times in the 155-day study period did the three papers agree on the most important story of the day—and those were, invariably and unquestionably the truly big stories of early 1977, at home and abroad: arms talks with Russia, the devastating winter in the East, the Canary Islands jet crash that killed more than 300 people, the Hanafi Muslims' takeover of three buildings in Washington, elections in Israel and India, conflict in Uganda and Zaire, the inauguration, appointments and programs of President Carter.
- On 56 days—one-third of the time—each of the three papers had a different lead story; that's twice as many days of complete disagreement as there were of complete agreement.
- 20 percent of the time—33 days—there was not one single story

that appeared on the front page of all three papers—and on only 32 days did the three front pages have more than two stories in common.

Shaw said that a separate study of newspapers in more than a dozen other cities on 50 days showed an even greater divergence in page-1 selection. A major reason for this, Shaw noted, is that most newspapers emphasize local news on their front pages and, except for the *New York Times, Washington Post,* and *Los Angeles Times,* "seem especially indifferent to all but the most cosmic foreign news events."

NEWSWORTHY ELEMENTS

The variables in time and judgments of journalists and readers are critical to the question of what news is. Although the amount and variety of news available to a modern newspaper and broadcast station are as unlimited as life itself, the media's capacity to present the news is rigidly restricted. A newspaper has just so many pages; a radio or television station has just so much air time. Therefore, news editors *must* be selective. They must judge each event and decide whether, in their minds, the event is worth reporting to the public, hoping all the while that the public agrees. Would the event be "interesting" to a large number of people? For every story included, a dozen, a hundred, perhaps a thousand must be excluded. By the same token, these judgments dètermine whether a selected event rates a long story on the front page or a brief mention buried on an inside page.

In making such judgments, an editor looks for certain elements or qualities that he thinks make some stories more compelling than others at a particular time. The relative value of the elements depends on the nature of the story and the views of the editor. In most stories the elements overlap. There is no set list, but most editors look for one or more of the following qualities:

Timeliness. News has always been a perishable commodity. Few people are interested in yesterday's news, especially now that radio and television provide instantaneous reporting.

Therefore, all factors being equal, immediacy probably will give one story the edge over another. Today's fire is likely to get priority over yesterday's robbery—on the assumption that readers and listeners already know about the robbery.

Immediacy applies not only to the time of occurence of an event, but also the time of discovery or disclosure. Such was the case, for example, with the story of the My Lai massacre in the Vietnam War. The incident, in which nearly all Vietnamese civilians in a village were deliberately killed, was kept secret by the United States government until investigative reporters discovered documents in Pentagon files long after the event occurred. The disclosure was front-page news. Similarly, prehistoric bones may lie hidden by time in East Africa; the existence of the bones is not a new happening; but the *discovery* of the bones is news.

Nowadays newspaper editors often pay less attention to the timeliness and more to the significance of a story. This is because the print media, with their production time lag between event and publication, cannot hope to beat the broadcast media in reporting spot news first.

It is not unusual for some newspapers to hold stories until more background details and interpretive material can be added or until the full story can be prepared. Such was the case with the *New York Times* disclosure of the Pentagon Papers about United States involvement in Vietnam. The *Times* did not rush into print as soon as it had most of the 47 volumes of the papers; instead, the editors held back until a special team, in a hushed operation, sifted through the material for six weeks in a rented hotel suite. The chance the *Times* took with the delay, of course, was that none of its competitors would also obtain the material and print it in the meantime.

Proximity. The closer the event, the greater is the interest. People can identify with news if they know the persons, conditions, or localities involved. They are more concerned about an explosion in their own community than an earthquake in another nation. A local election commands more attention than a state election in another part of the country.

An editor is always looking for the "local" angle. An accident in another community has a higher news value if one of the victims was a resident of the paper's town. If the state announces new financial aid to a number of communities, an editor is more likely to run the story if his town is a recipient than if it is not.

Conflict. People have always been interested in wars and other confrontations. There are countless variations: man versus man, man versus animal, man versus nature, nation versus nation.

Prominence. Well-known persons, places, and things always excite the curiosity of readers and listeners. When the governor arrives in town, he rates a story, whereas John Smith on the same plane is ignored. It may be news if a man jumps from a hotel window, but it's bigger news if he jumps from the Washington Monument.

Consequence. Happenings that directly affect the lives of his audience are usually reported by an editor. Examples are a breakdown of waterworks machinery, causing disruption of water flow to local homes; the City Council's passage of a new property tax, and a strike at a plant that employs many town workers. In a broader sense, examples include a scientific breakthrough that will improve the treatment of a common disease, or a problem with the Brazilian coffee crop that will mean more expensive coffee for American consumers. Other factors being equal, the news value is greater if the happening affects 100 percent of the audience than if it affects only 10 percent.

Magnitude. It is human nature that the interest of people seems to increase with the size of the event. Stronger news treatment is given to a traffic accident that kills ten persons than one with a single fatality; to a flood that devastates a ten-square-mile area than one that overruns a city block; to the city's purchase of fifty snow plows than the purchase of two.

Other Elements. Among other considerations are oddity (the familiar man-bites-dog concept) and human interest that excites the emotions (sex, helplessness, loneliness, injustice, humor, brutality).

Many studies have been made of news selection patterns, and journalists and readers have generally been found to be in substantial agreement as to their element preferences. Aside from timeliness and proximity, the factors that tend to elicit most interest are consequence and conflict.

INCREASE IN FEATURE STORIES

The rise of broadcast news has led the print media to expand their offerings of feature stories that do not depend for appeal on fast-breaking developments. In a rapidly changing world, the print media see a new job to be done, and the premise is that newspapers and magazines can perform this job better than the broadcast media can. The features are current, but not necessarily immediate, and can be read at the reader's leisure. As so often happens in the competitive news business, the success of features in the print media has led to more features in the broadcast media. The result is that the definition of newsworthiness has been broadened.

Human Interest. One class of feature getting increasing attention is the human-interest story. It exploits the old journalism axiom that people make news. Now commonplace, for instance, are tales about a day in the life of a hospital worker and new careers for retired people. Sections devoted to culture, sports, family and leisure activities, and how-to tips have been enlarged by most newspapers.

The interest in personalities has led to gossipy new magazines such as *People* and *Us*, "people" columns in newspapers, and expanded talk shows on radio and television. This same interest assured front-page play for such stories as Representative Wayne Hays's dalliance with a Capitol Hill office worker. All of which prompted the *Columbia Journalism Review* to observe about news judgment that the 1970s were slightly reminiscent of the 1920s era of "ballyhoo" journalism.

"Sidebars." Another newer type of feature includes the interpretive article, the backgrounder, and the person-in-the-news biography that usually supplements a breaking story. The main spot story provides an overall picture of a situation, touching at least briefly on many aspects of the story; the feature, called a "sidebar," goes into detail about one aspect considered especially important by the editors. Sidebars are intended to provide judgment and balance to the news, to give the reader deeper insight to the forces acting on the breaking news.

One example of a sidebar is an expert's analysis of various

political groups involved in a revolt in South America. It explains the philosophies, goals, and strengths of the groups, describes the groups' leaders, and puts the current revolt into historical perspective. While these points likely would be noted in the main story, there would not be enough room for details.

Another example is a short biography of a new Secretary of the Treasury. The main story would report the announcement by the President, a few major facts about the appointee, the circumstances that led to the appointment, and some indication of whether the appointment might lead to change in Treasury Department policies. The sidebar would produce a word picture of the appointee: personal appearance, professional experience, age and education, family and hobbies, likes and dislikes, views on his new job.

Sidebar features often are the result of weeks of investigation by teams of reporters. Editors sometimes anticipate news developments, assign investigative reporters to explore conditions expected to provoke the development, and then hold the sidebar until the breaking news actually comes. Or the procedure may be reversed. After the news development, the editor assigns the reporters to explore the conditions that led to the event.

Not surprisingly, broadcast stations have followed suit with their own efforts at interpretation. These efforts take the form of short supplementary material aired with the report on a breaking news story, or long documentaries on such subjects as hunger or migrant workers.

Crusades. Long a staple of newspapers, the crusade story (or series of stories) in the name of community service continues to be popular. These stories usually are not pegged to spot news, but they are newsworthy in that they describe and explain conditions that the newspaper believes should get attention. In a sense, the newspaper "makes" the news. The goal may be almost anything, from better housing or a new school to a crime-prevention program or antipollution measures.

DIFFERENCES IN APPROACH

The determination of newsworthiness also depends to a degree on the general approach, or emphasis, favored by a newspaper or broadcast station. The *New York Times*, which is almost a national newspaper, the *Washington Post,* the *Los Angeles Times,* and the broadcast networks carry considerable amounts of news of national and international importance, especially of politics and government, economics and social issues originating in Washington. Regional papers such as the *Minneapolis Star and Tribune,* and medium-sized broadcast stations, concentrate on news of their own city and surrounding states. Most smaller papers and stations lean almost entirely to local news. Within these broad contexts the news elements have varying importance to a specific editor.

CRITICISM OF NEWS SELECTION

A longstanding criticism of the media is that they carry too much bad news at the expense of the good. Critics say—and some newspeople agree—that the media fill their pages and air time with stories of crime, corruption, violence, disaster, war, unemployment, and tax increases and that they pay insufficient attention to achievements and triumphs. The criticism was particularly loud during the 1960s and early '70s, a period that included Vietnam, the youth revolt, and Watergate.

Many answers have been suggested. The media merely mirror society. It is a matter of perspective, and whether news is good or bad is in the eye of the beholder. The media *do* report much good news—such as scientific discoveries, space triumphs, cultural events, educational progress, environmental cleanup, success stories, and the routine of weddings, sports, and social activities. The trend toward "soft" service features and consumer guides in the "living" sections has added more "news" of a positive nature.

Perhaps the easiest, and most honest, answer is that the average reader and listener seem to be more interested in bad news than good. They want to know about events that deviate from the norm, that disrupt the stability of daily living. Obeying the law and living free of disaster are the norm for the majority of people; disobeying the law and getting hurt in an accident or a storm or demonstration are not. Some newspapers and television stations have experimented with special emphasis on "good" news and have found through audience surveys and sales that, in general, the public wasn't really interested.

On May 16, 1969, the *Miami News* deliberately omitted any story involving violence. It was a particularly telling experiment because a short time before the paper's deadline a Miami fugitive sought for murdering a policeman was captured in a shoot-out. It was the most dramatic running local story in weeks, but the *News* did not print a word about it. Its lead story was about a garbage strike.

Explaining the experiment on page 1, *News* editor Sylvan Meyer wrote: "This de-emphasis of violence for this one day may demonstrate that we, as readers, would not receive from our paper an accurate and complete picture of the world around us if the paper practiced such deliberate selectivity every day and tried to shield us from reality. . . ."

The bottom-line question is whether the media should provide what the average consumer wants or what the editors think the consumer should have to keep up with the world's major issues and questions. Many newspapers and broadcast stations do try to give their audiences a balanced ration of news, including important, often dull stories, whether the audiences like them or not; and they have the resources to survive, even thrive. Other newspapers and stations, recognizing that the media must make a profit to stay in business, are guided by the apparent interests of the audiences and provide the kinds of news that the average consumer is willing to pay for.

In the 1970s the balance seemed to be shifting clearly to reader and listener/viewer interests. The change suggested a modification of the definition of news to include any information that a reasonably large number of people want to be told.

NOTES

1. David Shaw, *Los Angeles Times* Syndicate, printed in the *Boston Globe*, June 28, 1977, p. 19.

SUGGESTED READING

Dexter, Lewis A., and White, David M., eds. *People, Society and Mass Communications*. New York: Free Press, 1964.

Nimmo, Dan D. *Newsgathering in Washington*. New York: Atherton, 1964.

Rochco, Bernard. *Newsmaking*. Chicago: University of Chicago Press, 1975.

Schramm, Wilbur. *Men, Messages and Media*. New York: Harper and Row, 1973.

3

A Brief History of the Media

The nature of news depends on the era and milieu. The news media reflect the society in which they operate. Both the news and the media are shaped by such factors as the state of education, size of communities, democratization of society, progress in transportation and communications technology, and rate of industrialization. Since America's beginning, newspapers have been the foremost agent for news presentation, augmented by magazines and later the broadcast media.

America's press grew out of the tradition and patterns existing in Britain and other European countries in the seventeenth century. From the slim journals of colonial times, the media have gone through eras of political control, personal journalism, and big business until today they are a vast interrelated network. The system's biggest transformation has come in the last half-century.

THE COLONIAL PERIOD, 1690–1776

The first newspaper attempted in the American colonies was *Publick Occurrences Both Foreign and Domestick*, a small three-pager printed in Boston by Benjamin Harris in 1690. It lasted only one issue because Harris failed to obtain a required license and the paper's contents offended the British authorities.

The spread of knowledge was seen as a threat to the people holding power, and the press was tolerated only as a servant in the interests of the government. The colonial governors, as representatives of the British Crown, had the right to control the press accordingly, and their heavy hand slowed the growth of newspapers. The rulers' attitude was typified by the Virginia governor's oft-quoted remark: "I thank God we have no free schools nor printing, and I hope we shall not have these hundred years. For learning has brought disobedience and heresy and sects into the world, and printing has divulged them and libels against the government. God keep us from both."

First Regular Weeklies. It was not until 1704 that the first regular weekly, *Boston News-Letter*, was put out by the postmaster, John Campbell. It displayed "Published by Authority" at the top, was dull, and attracted few readers or advertisers. The first criticism of constituted authority began to creep into the press with the *New England Courant*, started by James Franklin, whose younger brother Ben was a printer's apprentice and writer. The *Courant* gained popular support, including some influential men, and managed to survive despite its critical bent.

The first colonial newspapers, usually published by the local postmaster or a local printer, were simply extensions of person-to-person contact and community bulletin boards. They were directed mainly at an elite segment of society, those who could afford to buy papers and had the education to read them. The papers were published in the port towns and did not reach the majority of the population, which was dispersed and engaged primarily in agriculture. The news was of a merchandising nature (ships' arrivals and their cargoes) mixed with information reprinted from British newspapers brought in by ship. The stories generally were selected and colored to promote special interests supported by the publishers.

As rebellious feelings against Britain began to mount, some newspapers openly protested impositions from London such as the Trades Acts and the Stamp Act; other papers, opposing revolt against constituted authority, sided with England. When the

Revolutionary War started in 1775, the public and press fervor increased, and pro-Patriot journalists helped rally both troops and people to the anti-British cause. Newspapers fluctuated in number during the fighting, but by war's end in 1783, there were about 35 and the press's place in the New World had been established.

Pamphleteering. A popular and prominent journalistic device in the controversies was pamphleteering, with Thomas Paine a leading writer on behalf of independence. Paine wrote his famous *Common Sense* in early 1776, and later his *Crisis* papers. The first paper, printed in the pro-Patriot *Pennsylvania Journal*, included the long-remembered line, "These are the times that try men's souls."

The Stamp Act. A key factor in the independence movement, and an important victory for the colonial press, was the successful fight against the 1765 Stamp Act. Intended by Britain as one effort to replenish its treasury depleted by the long war against France, this act levied taxes on, among other things, newsprint. Such a tax had long been imposed on newspapers in Britain and other European countries, but many colonial publishers fought it on grounds that it infringed on their freedom. Their newspapers printed protest letters and other attacks on the tax, and in less than a year Parliament repealed that part of the Act that applied to printers.

An interesting side effect of the newspaper tax was that it apparently was responsible for the size of pages since used by the press. The tax was imposed on the basis of each page, regardless of the page size. The earliest newspapers had book-size pages; but when the tax was enforced, publishers soon recognized that they could print more information at lower cost if they switched to large pages. As time went by, printing equipment was designed to accommodate the large pages and, though considered unwieldly by many people, the large pages are still used by most of the world's newspapers.

The Zenger Case. During the colonial period, the landmark trial of John Peter Zenger, publisher of the *New York Weekly Journal*, set a foundation for establishing the legal rights of a free press to say what it wants. Zenger, who sided with a political faction opposed to the royal governor, was arrested in 1734 on charges of seditious libel. His lawyer, Andrew Hamilton, challenged the English law that "the greater the truth the greater the libel," arguing that printing the truth was not criminally libelous. Hamilton also argued that a jury, not a governor, should decide whether a publication was libelous.

The chief justice denied Hamilton on both counts, but the jury acquitted Zenger, even though the verdict went against existing law. Since that time, Zenger's name has been linked with press freedom because the two principles introduced at his trial gradually gained acceptance and later were formalized into law and practice.

Magazines. Magazines were slower than newspapers to develop. They did not deal with news, but mainly with literary and practical arts. Magazine reading was a leisure-time activity for the upper classes, and much of the material came from London. Printing was difficult, subscribers and advertisers were limited, and few magazines lasted very long. The first two magazines appeared in 1741: The *General Magazine, and Historical Chronicle, for All the British Plantations in America*, issued by Benjamin Franklin; and the *American Magazine, or a Monthly View of the Political State of the British Colonies*, published by Andrew Bradford, Philadelphia's official printer. *General Magazine* lasted six months; *American Magazine* only three.

THE PARTY PRESS, 1776–1835

The partisan flavor of the late colonial years carried over into the post-Revolutionary period. Along with the lingering quarrels among the thirteen states over such issues as boundary lines, currencies, and interstate commerce, there were the large problems involved in establishing nationhood and securing independence. With the people deeply divided, these matters provided plenty of grist for the growing number of newspapers, as politicians maneuvered for power in the new government. The emphasis was on persuasion rather than objective news reporting. What little news was included continued to be mainly reprinted information from British newspapers.

Politics and Debate. Because at this time the concept of press freedom did not include responsibility to the public, little thought was given to accuracy and fairness in the newspapers. The papers were supported largely by political subsidies, and they became forums for contending politicians to publicize their views through editorials and pen-name letters. Propaganda notwithstanding, the newspapers were a principal means whereby the keenest minds of the period debated key issues confronting the emerging nation.

The biggest issue was the degree of centrality of power. The Federalists, led by Alexander Hamilton, favored a strong central government based primarily on the judgments of public officials; the Republicans, or anti-Federalists, whose spokesman was Thomas Jefferson, believed that power should be dispersed among the states, with more reliance on the judgment of the electorate. Out of this debate came the famous *Federalist Papers*, a series of letters written by Hamilton, James Madison, and John Jay, that were widely printed in newspapers in 1787 and 1788.

Liberty and License. The struggle carried on in the press was bitter and, as one history of the period puts it, "freedom from government control resulted in as much license as liberty." Scant effort was made to curb lies, libel, and vitriol. None of the leaders escaped attack, a condition that led Jefferson, in a reversal of his earlier feelings, to write disgustedly in a letter to a friend: "The man who never looks into a paper is better informed than he who reads them."

In this environment, the early Presidents—notably George Washington, John Adams, Jefferson, and later Andrew Jackson —sought to "manage" the news of government, if not control or suppress it. On the one hand they recognized that if they were to have popular support, the people had to be informed of what they were doing; on the other hand they wanted the released information to reflect credit on their administrations. This was best achieved by favoring their own party newspapers as the dominant sources of presidential news.

Weeklies and Dailies. The early newspapers were weeklies; it was not until 1783 that the first daily was started, a conversion of the weekly *Pennsylvania Evening Post*. Others followed quickly in New York, Baltimore, and Charleston. Then a surge of new papers after the turn of the century raised the number of both weeklies and dailies to several hundred, approximately 75 of them dailies. These papers still were geared and priced for the elite mercantile and political classes.

Decline and Change. As a result of a combination of circumstances, the party press began to decline soon after Jackson's presidency. Many of the newspapers were now relatively influential. The transmission of information, long dependent on transportation such as ships and horses, took a big leap forward with the invention of the telegraph. With the expanding system of education, more Americans had become readers, and their horizons had been extended by the steamship and railroad.

These changes encouraged large circulations and increased advertising, made possible by printing improvements such as the high-speed press. With more advertising revenues, and lower costs for printing, publishers could depend less on political subsidies. This change coincided with a series of Presidents after Jackson (Van Buren, Harrison, Tyler, Polk) who were less adept at trying to manage the news printed in the press. As a result of all these factors, political control of newspapers waned.

Magazines. In the post–Revolutionary War period magazines were still few and had no real role in the political skirmishes. Helped by the Postal Act of 1794, which permitted them to be carried in the mails, magazines began to progress in both number and quality around the turn of the century. Many attracted the best writers and editors. The dominant format in the early part of the century was information and instruction about special interests of specific new audiences—farmers, teachers, professional people, historians.

By 1825 only about 100 magazines were stable enough for continuing publication, but the medium was approaching an era of expansion. The new public consciousness of an independent nation, the spread of education, the growth of cities, and the improvement of printing created the potential for mass marketing of magazines.

PERSONAL JOURNALISM, 1835–1900

Modern newspaper history began in the early 1830s. The new environment was conducive to cheap newspapers with popular appeal. Sensing an expanding and profitable market, publishers changed the format and content and lowered the price of their papers. Dailies were added to the weeklies. Within just a few years the press went from small upper-class readership to mass readership, and newspapers burgeoned spectacularly both in number and in circulation.

During this period the press shifted from political to private control, and its emphasis became "objective" news rather than partisan opinion. The dominant figures in the transformation were such journalistic giants as James Gordon Bennett, Horace Greeley, Joseph Pulitzer, and William Randolph Hearst.

Penny Press. Most post–Revolutionary newspapers sold for six cents, which only the elite could afford. There were a few abortive attempts to publish at lower prices, but the first to succeed was by a young printer named Benjamin H. Day. In 1833 Day launched the *New York Sun* and sold it for a penny, counting on a mass demand to bring him adequate financial return. To give the *Sun* popular appeal, he cut back on dull political reports and concentrated on sprightly written human-interest news of the streets and the common man. He paid the first press attention to such things as police-court activities and suicides. The formula worked: the *Sun*'s circulation shot up immediately. It was the beginning of the penny press.

James Gordon Bennett. Of all the imitators of Day's formula, James Gordon Bennett did most to enlarge upon it with his *New York Herald*, started in 1835. Bennett set the pattern for the penny press and newspapers of the future. He stated his policy in his first issue: "We shall support no party, be the organ of no faction or coterie, and care nothing for any election or any candidate from President down to constable. We shall endeavor to record facts, on every public and proper subject, stripped of verbiage and coloring, with comments suitable, just, independent, fearless and good-tempered. . . ."

Aiming at mass appeal, the flamboyant and talented Bennett at first focused on sensationalized local news written in a terse, blunt style. Then, drawing on his experience as Washington correspondent, reporter, and editor, he branched into national and international news. He is credited with such innovations as Wall Street coverage, "beat-type" reporting in the city, national correspondents in strategically located cities, a Washington bureau to cover the capital, a staff of foreign correspondents, and the concept of "getting the news first." He was one of the pioneer crusaders, always siding with the have-nots, and was often brutal in his attacks. A shrewd businessman, Bennett built the *Herald* into the most informative newspaper of the period, with a circulation of 60,000.

Later, Bennett's son, James, Jr., took over the *Herald* and added a new twist: to encourage readership, he initiated stunts, or made newsworthy events happen. It was young Bennett who sent English journalist Henry Morton Stanley to Africa in search of David Livingstone. Stanley wrote a series of widely read stories about his mission, which included one of history's famous remarks: "Doctor Livingstone, I presume?"

Horace Greeley. If the Bennetts emphasized information, Horace Greeley emphasized influence. His *New York Tribune*, started in 1841, was the prototype of the "personal journalism" reflecting a newspaper proprietor's personal views (and sometimes his eccentricities) that prevailed during the remainder of the century. Though the daily *Tribune* did not match Bennett's *Herald* in circulation, it was considered the country's most influential newspaper. Greeley himself was one of the best-known Americans of the time, although he espoused some radical causes and often was inconsistent in his stands.

Greeley minimized the trivialities of the penny press, believing it was the responsibility of a newspaper to provide political and moral leadership through serious discussion, interpretation of events, and editorial argument. He assembled an able news-gathering staff, but his hard-hitting editorials for reform were the heart of his publication. The *Herald* was the first American newspaper to develop an editorial page.

Mid-century America was fertile for Greeley's kind of newspapering. It was changing from an agricultural to an industrial society, with all the dislocations and injustices that such a transition creates. Among Greeley's favorite targets were slavery and capital punishment, which he opposed; and labor unions, equal suffrage for women, and western expansion of the nation ("Go west, young man"), which he backed.

Mass Circulation. The penny press with mass circulation (mass at that time meant 10,000 to 20,000 copies sold) was well established in the cities by mid-century, and newspapers continued to grow in number, size, and profits as the Civil War approached. Weeklies still were the most numerous, but by the time the war started in 1861 there were about 400 dailies. Newsgathering and production techniques improved steadily, especially under the pressures of covering the war.

After the war, and continuing to 1900, there was a spurt in population, education, industrialization, urbanization, national wealth, and communications technology. The changes resulted in social, political, and economic unrest, and new interest in reform movements, science, literature, and education. Consumer goods now mass-produced by the new industries created increased demands for newspaper advertising.

These conditions spurred development of the press into a capitalistic industry involving fierce competition for circulation, advertising, and profits. The main contestants for circulation, and the dominant figures of the press near the turn of the century, were Joseph Pulitzer and William Randolph Hearst.

Joseph Pulitzer. Joseph Pulitzer founded the *St. Louis Post-Dispatch* in 1878 and soon had it thriving. He combined an aggressive, crusading editorial page with thorough news coverage that included some sensationalism for mass appeal. In 1883 Pulitzer bought the *New York World*, assembled an able staff, and repeated the formula—with added touches.

The *World* started the first sports section and comics, brightened the pages with illustrations, and crusaded against greedy monopolists and bribe-taking government officials. The sex and crime on the front page were for the masses, the exposés and editorial page for more serious readers. Within just a few years after Pulitzer bought it, the *World* was putting out morning, evening, and Sunday editions with an extensive combined circulation and a highly profitable advertising volume.

William Randolph Hearst. Pulitzer's success caught the eye of young William Randolph Hearst, who applied the Pulitzer formula to his father's *San Francisco Examiner*. Then Hearst bought the *New York Journal* in 1895 and, with a family fortune behind him, set out to overtake Pulitzer.

Hearst hired away some of the best reporters and editors from the *World* and other papers. He enlarged the use of photography and introduced color printing to newspapers, both of which had popular appeal. He borrowed the sensationalism of Bennett and Pulitzer, and the crusading editorializing of Pulitzer, and expanded on them boldly.

Yellow Journalism. The circulation race led to abundant stories about sin and corruption, sensational pictures, and expanded use of popular comics. To attract customers, both the *World* and the *Journal* engaged in shrill debate and jingoistic coverage of the Spanish-American War. This emphasis on sensationalism came to be known as "yellow journalism," a term taken from a comic strip called "The Yellow Kid" (the Kid's costume was yellow).

Extras. The methods and contents of the Pulitzer and Hearst papers in New York influenced the development of other newspapers in the East. Outside the East the press was less activist, the interests were local or regional, and community service was a dominant feature. A leading paper outside the East was Joseph Medill's *Chicago Tribune*.

Most large cities by now had competing daily newspapers that depended heavily on street sales. It was during this time that "extras" and "bulletins" were started on the assumption that the latest news would boost street circulation. The practice was facilitated by the emerging use of the telephone by journalists. Striving to be first with the news became a newspaper tradition that endured until electronic media provided instantaneous reporting.

Objectivity. The drive for large circulation was a major factor in another durable press tradition: objectivity as a reporting standard. The newspapers wanted to win customers of all stripes, not repulse them with partisan opinion or one-sided stories. Editors therefore began to include news aimed at "the lowest common denominator"—a philosophy fostered later by the press associations. To avoid offending readers, all sides were represented; and if viewpoints were unavoidable, they were balanced as much as possible.

The swing to objectivity marked the beginning of the "democratization" of news. Targeting news at the masses to increase circulation meant that the common man's interests and tastes largely determined the content of newspapers. Thus, while objectivity has come to be looked upon as a quality that a free press should have, the original and persistent impetus was more economic than idealistic or journalistic.

Magazines. What has been called a "golden age" of magazines also emerged from the societal changes after the Civil War.

Publishers such as S. S. McClure, Frank Munsey, and Cyrus Curtis were leaders in introducing magazines of low price, popular appeal, and national circulation. The transformation to a mass medium was made possible by better printing methods, a bigger readership with education and more leisure time, railroads that permitted wide distribution, and increased advertising for mass-produced goods.

Some of the more enduring literary and opinion magazines were started during this period: *Harper's Monthly, Atlantic Monthly, Nation, Century*. In the mass-circulation field were *Ladies' Home Journal, Saturday Evening Post, Collier's, Munsey's, McClure's*, and *Cosmopolitan*.

BIG BUSINESS JOURNALISM, 1900–1945

Early in the twentieth century, opinion and political party ties were subordinated even more to the newsgathering function. Sensationalism faded (though it reappeared during the "Roaring Twenties"). This transition was epitomized by the development of the *New York Times* as a newspaper devoted to, as it said, "All the News That's Fit to Print." Great changes were taking place in the world, and the public wanted to know about them: economic and political reform in the United States, World War I and the postwar period of adjustment, the Depression, and a collapse of world order that led to World War II.

By now, running a large-city newspaper was expensive, and most had become corporate enterprises. The period between 1900 and World War II saw the growth of newspaper chains, the emergence of the news wire services, newsmagazines and radio, the birth of some of the most notable magazines, and the heyday of muckraking.

The New York Times. Symbolic of the trend toward acceptance of the news-function responsibility was the development of the *New York Times*. Adolph S. Ochs bought the *Times* in 1896 at the height of the Pulitzer-Hearst circulation war and, maintaining a sober approach to the news, offered what a large segment of the public clearly wanted. The paper's circulation grew, and so did its strength and influence. The *Times* rates special attention because it became a standard model in American journalism.

The *Times*, founded in 1851 by Henry J. Raymond, was light

on partisanship and heavy on principle. In its pursuit of the broadest possible coverage of news and promotion of community welfare, it offered an option, as John Tebbel puts it in *The Media in America*, to Bennett's "sensationalism and cynical views" and Greeley's "liberal high-mindedness."[1] The *Times* had gained attention and applause for its exposé of the Tweed Ring political scandal, but was faltering financially when Ochs took it over.

Stating that "it will be my aim . . . to give the news impartially, without fear or favor," Ochs shunned yellow journalism and chose to leave out comics and other entertainment features adopted by many papers as inducements to circulation. Instead, he and his editor, Carr V. Van Anda, concentrated on persistent and comprehensive coverage of significant national and international events. The reporting was objective, the tone somber, the contents thorough to the point that the *Times* became known as a "newspaper of record."

Ochs laid the foundation, and his successors built on it, for a newspaper that grew into one of the world's most stable, durable, respected, and influential. It became standard reading for diplomats, government officials, and the intelligentsia, and a ready reference in libraries for academicians, students, and other researchers. Its forte continued to be coverage of national and international news, exceeding that of other newspapers in quantity if not always in quality.

Over the years the *Times* adjusted, sometimes slowly and reluctantly, to what its leaders considered the changing needs and interests of the reading public by extensive coverage of special fields such as science and education, interpretation of the news, and, more recently, expanded coverage of lifestyles and leisure-time activities.

Although it has maintained high standards, emulated widely throughout journalism, the *Times* has not been uncriticized. Rightly or wrongly, it has been accused at various times of neglecting the little man; or being pompous and bland ("the good gray lady"), and of being insufficiently selective to the point of overwhelming the average reader (for example, the average size of the Sunday edition in recent years has been over 500 pages; the record on October 17, 1965, contained 946 pages weighing 7.8 pounds).

Other Leading Newspapers. The *New York Times* was only one of many newspapers that grew into significant journalistic institutions during the first half of the twentieth century. In New York there were the *Herald Tribune,* the *Post,* the *World-Telegram and Sun,* the *Daily News,* and the *Daily Mirror.* Elsewhere the highly regarded papers included, to name a few, the *Washington Post,* the *Baltimore Sun,* the *Louisville Courier-Journal,* the *Tribune* and the *Daily News* in Chicago, the *St. Louis Post-Dispatch,* the *Kansas City Star,* the *Milwaukee Journal,* the *Minneapolis Star and Tribune,* the *Des Moines Register,* the *Denver Post,* and the *Los Angeles Times.* Some of these were amalgams of earlier papers.

Newspaper Chains. By the early twentieth century competition among newspapers was so keen (in New York City there were 14), and their operating costs were so high, that the press came increasingly under the dominance of businessmen-publishers with corporate backing. Starting after the Civil War, with industrialization and urbanization, circulations began to climb and readers demanded efficient and expanded services. This meant that newspapers needed capital for equipment and higher operating costs. Many papers could not find the money and, unable to compete, were forced to fold or to consolidate with one or more other papers. These conditions created the milieu for the beginning of chain publishing, whereby several newspapers were owned and operated by one publisher or publishing corporation. From a peak of 2,460 in 1916, the number of newspapers began a decline after World War I that continued to mid-century, when it leveled off.

The first American to make chain publishing work successfully was E. W. Scripps, who established what later became the Scripps-Howard chain of major newspapers around the country, plus smaller chains in Michigan and the Northwest and on the Pacific Coast. William Randolph Hearst was the other giant of the chains; by 1931 he had taken 42 dailies under his wing.

Tabloids. The "Roaring Twenties" or "Jazz Age" that followed World War I brought a revival of sensational journalism in the form of tabloids, patterned after the successful *Daily Mirror* in London. With pages half the size of conventional newspapers, and aimed at the blue-collar masses, the tabloids featured sex and crime, eye-catching photographs, and large headlines.

The *New York Daily News*, started by Joseph M. Patterson in 1919, went to a million circulation within six years. Since then it has maintained the largest circulation (2 million in the mid-1970s) of any American paper, although it has leavened its sex and crime with more serious news. There were several imitators, notably Hearst's *Mirror* in New York, but none has had the staying power of the *Daily News*.

Press Associations. Known also as wire services, press associations grew out of the demand for national and international news, and the inability of individual newspapers to cover much news outside their local areas. Few newspapers could afford to station correspondents in Washington and abroad, much less the various regions of the United States. The press associations filled the gap with cooperative newsgathering and distribution by telegraph or leased wires.

Three wire services dominated the field in the United States. The Associated Press (AP), which was started in 1848 by New York City newspapers to pool shipping news, expanded greatly after 1900. The United Press (UP) was founded by Scripps in 1907, and two years later the International News Service (INS) was started by Hearst. In 1958 UP and INS merged to make United Press International (UPI). The evolution of the wire services greatly enlarged the media's scope of news coverage.

Newsmagazines. These weeklies were a natural by-product of the proliferation of news and growing audiences in the first half of the twentieth century. They offered a mixture of news summary, interpretation, and opinion. They were intended to service people too busy to peruse the other media, subscribers wishing to augment the limited coverage of local newspapers, and anyone interested in a sophisticated approach to news interpretation and opinion.

Henry Luce launched *Time* in 1923 with a format that departmentalized subject matter into national affairs, foreign affairs, business, science, education, religion, books, theater, and others as time went by. *Newsweek* appeared a decade later with a similar format. *U.S. News & World Report*, which followed in a few years, used roughly the same approach, but in a less structured format. *Life* and *Look*, started in the 1930s, were basically general-interest picture magazines, but they offered highlights of the week's news.

Radio. Though viewed as an entertainment medium, radio confronted newspapers with new competition in the years leading up to and during World War II. Radio's news offerings were limited, but they added a fresh dimension to the communication experience: by the simple flip of a dial, listeners could be involved vicariously in events taking place thousands of miles away. Radio also meant that people could hear the news before it was printed, because radio reported news immediately and directly whereas printed news required hours to produce and distribute. This development killed the newspaper "extra," the special edition put out hurriedly to announce a big event, and caused a reduction in the number of daily editions published by the metropolitan papers.

The first real tinkering with gadgets like the crystal set began right after World War I. By the mid-1920s, radio as a mass medium was picking up momentum. One of the first to recognize radio's potential was David Sarnoff, a former Marconi wireless operator who soon became a key figure in the Radio Corporation of America and its subsidiary, the National Broadcasting Company (NBC).

In the early 1920s local stations started broadcasting news summaries, usually in cooperation with affiliated newspapers. In 1926 NBC inaugurated the first network with 24 stations interconnected, and the next year the first coast-to-coast hookup (for a football game) was achieved. That same year the Columbia Broadcasting System (CBS) was organized, followed by the Mutual Broadcasting System six years later. For some years NBC operated two networks (Red and Blue) and so dominated national radio that it was forced by the Federal Communications Commission to give up one. In 1943, NBC sold the Blue Network, which became the American Broadcasting Company (ABC).

During the early years of radio, stations went on and off the air at will and wandered from frequency to frequency, often interfering with each other. To alleviate the chaos, Congress passed the Radio Act in 1927, giving the federal government power to regulate the number of broadcasting stations allowed. The Radio Act was amended in 1934 by the Communications Act, which created the Federal Communications Commission. The electromagnetic spectrum in the air was established as a national resource to be allocated and regulated, through the granting by the FCC of three-year licenses to stations.

Stabilization of the radio system led to growth and increased advertising, thus creating more of a challenge to the newspapers. One way that the newspapers sought to meet the challenge was to limit radio's access to news from the press associations. This situation lasted until the late 1930s, when a compromise was reached and the press associations began wire reports written especially for radio delivery.

In the meantime radio began attracting large national audiences with such popular programs as *Amos 'n' Andy* and such entertainers as Jack Benny, Kate Smith, and Burns and Allen. Interest in instantaneous, on-the-spot news reports was whetted by events such as the Lindbergh kidnap trial in 1934, presidential nominating conventions, the abdication of King Edward VIII, and President Franklin D. Roosevelt's "fireside chats." Before long the names of radio commentators (H. V. Kaltenborn, Lowell Thomas, Gabriel Heatter) were household words. Radio news came of age during World War II, starting with the Munich crisis in 1939, with direct reports from the fronts and human-interest impressions from European capitals, such as Edward R. Murrow's *This Is London.*

The decade between 1935 and 1945 was a period of remarkable growth for radio in technology, advertising revenues, and number of stations. By 1945 there were more than 900 commercial stations, with hundreds more preparing to operate or waiting for license approval. Daily newscasts were now an important part of the radio schedule, and the networks and most of the major stations had news staffs, including correspondents in key cities.

Even so, radio had little impact on the dominance and prosperity of newspapers in the news field. In the relatively short air time allotted to news as opposed to entertainment, radio offered only summaries, supplemented by brief commentaries; people still read newspapers to get the full stories. And when television arrived after World War II, radio's news role was eclipsed by broadcasting's new star.

General Magazines. The established magazines, especially the *Saturday Evening Post* and the *Ladies' Home Journal*, continued to grow, and some notable publications were added to the field. In the 1920s and 1930s, Harold Ross started the *New Yorker*, Dewitt Wallace created the *Reader's Digest*, Henry Luce launched *Fortune*, and H. L. Mencken and George Jean Nathan founded the *American Mercury*. All of these magazines had strong impact on America's reading habits and culture.

Muckraking. What came to be known as "muckraking" hit its zenith in magazines during the first decade of the twentieth century. The term, coined by President Theodore Roosevelt, was applied to a new kind of activist, in-depth reporting that went beyond previous crusading by the press. It was aimed at exposing corruption and other ills in society's institutions, and the practice was the forerunner of what later was called simply "investigative" reporting.

Muckraking grew out of the economic and social unheavals caused by industrialization. An expanding gap developed between the business and government "haves" and the "have not" masses whose education and upbringing left them unprepared for the rapid changes. The environment was fertile for corruption and exploitation. The first publication to recognize the journalistic and circulation possibilities was *McClure's*. Its immediate success soon drew others into the act.

There followed a wave of revelations about the monopolism of industrial barons, municipal corruption, patent-medicine abuses, insurance manipulations, and other ills. Among the prominent muckraking writers were Lincoln Steffens, Ida M. Tarbell, and Samuel Hopkins Adams. Their exposés appeared in such magazines as *McClure's, Colliers, Everybody's, Ladies' Home Journal, Cosmopolitan,* and *American.*

Muckraking articles proved to be popular reading among the masses for several years, and some reforms emerged as a result of new public pressures. Predictably, however, the exposés were unpopular with business interests that paid for magazine advertising, and after a decade publishers eased off on muckraking.

THE TELEVISION AGE, 1945—

After World War II, television invaded American homes and ignited a communications and information revolution. Although primarily an entertainment medium, TV also caught the public's fancy with its limited, on-the-spot presentation of news "as it happens." Stations and receiving sets proliferated, drawing to television large amounts of media advertising. These changes forced self-examination and modifications among the other media, resulting in a vast network of institutionalized and interlocking information outlets. The emergence of broadcasting and other technological developments, combined with a rapidly changing world and an increasingly sophisticated audience, brought about a dramatic transformation of the communications system.

Emergence of TV. After some experimentation in the 1920s and 1930s, television emerged on a commercial basis in the late 1940s. Equipment developed during World War II opened the way for a proliferation of stations and transcontinental transmission via coaxial cable. The technological growth was accompanied by national network programming designed for simultaneous presentation in living rooms across the land. To allow the FCC to work out a plan for equitable service nationwide, the federal government imposed a "freeze" on station authorizations in 1948. When the freeze ended four years later, the age of television began in earnest.

Television immediately caught the public imagination. People, like a child with a new toy, delighted in seeing "live" shows right in their living rooms. Watching TV became a social ritual, and the program schedule helped determine daily routines and lifestyles of millions of Americans. Contributing to the rapid rise of TV was its timing: it emerged at a moment in history when Americans were becoming more affluent, more mobile, and more fragmented in their family and social lives. The affluence enabled people to afford television, and the mobility and fragmentation deprived people of some traditional home and social activities. Evidence of TV's appeal was the fact that consumers had to make a sizable investment in special equipment to receive the medium's offerings—something they did not have to do with newspapers and magazines.

Purveyor of News. Although television, like radio, focused on entertainment to draw large audiences for advertising, making stars of such performers as Milton Berle, Ed Sullivan, and Howdy Doody, it also developed a significant impact as a purveyor of news. Television offered what newspapers could not: direct

witnessing of events on a screen as they took place, rather than
getting a secondhand written report. And TV took radio a big
step further, adding sight to sound. The introduction of color
in the 1950s was an appealing bonus.

By its nature, TV proved most effective in presenting dramatic and action-filled events: the Senate's Joseph McCarthy–
Army hearings in the early 1950s; space shots and man's walk
on the moon; the drama surrounding President Kennedy's
assassination; fighting in the Vietnam War; congressional hearings on the Watergate scandal; political conventions and debates (Chicago police clashing at the 1968 Democratic convention,
with demonstrators shouting, "The whole world is watching").

But the nightly newscasts, however restricted in their coverage,
also attracted large audiences; in the 1970s an estimated 41
million Americans watched the 7 o'clock news on the three networks. The faces of newscasters such as Walter Cronkite, Chet
Huntley, David Brinkley, John Chancellor, Howard K. Smith,
Harry Reasoner, and Barbara Walters became familiar in homes
across the nation. These newscasts were augmented by occasional
in-depth documentaries, taking the lead from the early *See It
Now* series of Edward R. Murrow and Fred W. Friendly that
exposed, among other things, the ills of McCarthyism and the
exploitation of migrant workers.

Expansion of Stations and Sets. As advertisers saw the allure
of television as a medium to reach consumers on a national basis,
the three networks (ABC, CBS, and NBC) shifted their emphasis
from radio to TV (Mutual elected to stay out of TV). They
produced slick and expensive programming designed to attract
the widest possible audiences—and thus advertising revenues.
At the same time, businessmen recognized the profit potential
of station ownership.

The result was a steady increase in both sending stations
(within the limitations of government regulation) and receiving
sets. In 1955 there were 439 commercial stations and 33 million
sets; within 20 years the numbers had grown to 953 stations and
112 million sets in 97 percent of American homes. During that
period TV sets had become more common in the United States
than automobiles and flush toilets.

Impact on Other Media. At first it was thought that the
popularity of television, and its appeal to advertisers, would

cause a decline in the other media; but generally this did not happen. Instead, the competitive stimulus created by TV forced the other media into modifications that led to more specific roles for which each was better suited. Television—because of its economic structure geared to high-cost production, and its news high points aside—remained rooted in entertainment as primarily a medium for marketing merchandise.

As it turned out, the glimpses of daily happenings offered by TV whetted the public's appetite for information that was more readily available in the print media. The emergence of television was a factor in the closing of some large-city newspapers, but other papers merged and new ones opened in the suburbs, with the result that the total number in the country remained steady. Largely because of their local dominance, daily newspapers still commanded the lion's share of advertising in the 1970s. Several mass-circulation general magazines, losing out to TV on national advertising and affected by rising postal rates, went out of business; but hundreds of specialized magazines sprang up in their place. Book publishers found that television stimulated, rather than discouraged, reading, and the paperback industry flourished. Radio stations shifted to a local emphasis with music, talk shows, and reports on consumer wants, weather, and traffic—a role generally unsuited to TV.

THE BIG TRANSFORMATION

Of all the eras of change for the American media, the period since World War II has brought the most dramatic transformation. The major overlapping factors in this transformation are discussed in the following sections.

Advances in Technology. Automation and the sophistication of communications technology have enlarged the reservoir of knowable information and facilitated the dissemination of this information among more people.

In the print media, the development of high-transmission methods and electronic processing has speeded up and expanded the gathering, storing, and transferring of words for newspapers, magazines, and books. Whereas teletype machines for years delivered news to newsrooms at an effective rate of about 45 words a minute, new models are capable of 1,000 words or more a minute. Current information or research material that had been recorded on paper stored in files, retrieved by hand, and transferred manually from office to office, can now go through the same process with computer data banks and electronic terminals that require a fraction of the time and manpower needed for the old method. Computerization and other electronic innovations have not only improved the quality of printing, but have also reduced the labor, time, and costs involved in setting lines of type and other steps of the production process.

In broadcasting, pocket transistors and car radios have expanded the scope and convenience of radio. Equipment modifications have improved television transmission and reception, and lowered prices of sets. Hand-held cameras (minicams) have given TV journalists mobility they did not have with their early bulky equipment. Journalists can now record with relative ease what is happening in an Asian village under attack, or on the floor of a political convention stirred by debate.

Videotape, which unlike film does not have to be processed, has simplified the delivery of motion pictures to the TV screen. Communications satellites and other technological marvels have enabled television to beam its pictures directly across oceans and continents without need of cables and land relay stations, over mountains into isolated regions once out of reach, and even from the moon and Mars.

Broadening of Interests. The increase in knowable information and the growing complexity of human relations have led to a broadening of interests among all peoples. And the exchange of ideas and information about these interests has been facilitated because most countries now have modern communications.

Jet planes and other transportation improvements have increased international travel, stimulating interest in foreign lands and peoples. Between 1955 and 1975, the annual number of Americans traveling abroad jumped from 1 million to 6 million. Journalists now can quickly jet into remote areas and send out reports of events and conditions that not many years ago went unnoticed by most of the world.

International relations that grew out of World War II, and the wave of African and Asian countries gaining independence, have created new concerns for Americans. The Vietnam War was an example. There have been realignments of economic power; societies have become interdependent; and events taking place in any society have become more relevant to peoples in other societies. (A meeting of Arab oil-producing nations, for instance, affects the price of gas for American cars.)

At the same time, as populations have grown and people have migrated to cities, living has become increasingly disorderly. There now are more problems and more conflicts for available food and resources. This trend has put new emphasis on such subjects as the economy, the environment, housing, employment, education, medical care, crime, discrimination against various groups, consumer protection, and scientific development. Add to this the historic trend toward more popular electoral forms of government across the world, a trend that cries out for quick and extensive exchanges of information and ideas.

Prominence of Broadcasting. The spread of radio and television, with their facility to reach larger audiences than any other medium, has affected the communication of information and ideas in two significant ways.

First, radio and the ubiquitous transistor have crossed political and geographic borders often closed to other media. This has increased the potential for interplay of information and ideas. For instance, radio stations in non-Communist countries have reached listeners in adjacent Communist countries where American newspapers and TV programs have not been available to the general public. Inexpensive transistors, used for educational purposes as well as news, are now fairly common in remote villages once cut off from the outside world.

Television has beamed into living rooms and classrooms pictures of places, people, and things that in the past have been unfamiliar to most Americans except in books or in the abstract. The evening newscast may show a protest demonstration by black miners in South Africa or the lifestyle of a primitive tribe in a Brazilian jungle or a new form of commuter transportation in Japan. The result is the availability of more information and increased interest in such information.

Second, the instantaneous, from-the-scene reporting of broadcasting has put new emphasis on audiovisual, as opposed to written, presentation of news. It also has made it impossible for print media to be first with the news, and has injected drama and listener/viewer involvement that are difficult for newspapers to duplicate. The print media therefore have been forced to seek new forms and approaches that are unfeasable for broadcasting. The most notable trend has been toward advocacy journalism and more interpretation and investigation to give meaning to news reported briefly, albeit first, on radio and television.

Change in Audience. On the whole, Americans have become better educated since World War II. They are more sophisticated about new and different ideas, younger, and increasingly more oriented to the electronic media than to the old-time newspaper. These characteristics have added up to an expanded appetite for information, with stress on the speed, drama, and action provided by broadcasting, but supplemented by the in-depth reporting, interpretation, and investigation provided by newspapers and magazines.

In 1940, in a total population of 132 million, the median number of school years completed among people of twenty-five years old and over was 8.6; in 1975, with a population of 213 million, the median was 12.3 years. In 1940, 24.5 percent of that age category had finished high school and 4.6 percent had four or more years of college; in 1975, the corresponding figures were 62.5 percent and 13.9 percent. As studies have shown, the acquisition of education usually generates a desire for information and news.

After the post–World War II baby boom, the percentage of young people in the national population grew, and a youth culture evolved. By the 1970s, half of all Americans were under twenty-five years old. As a group they were better off economically, as well as better educated and more sophisticated, than preceding generations. They were accustomed to rapid societal change. They had new interests that were reflected in their media preferences. Having grown up in a television age, they were attuned to broadcasting and thus were a major factor in the content and operational adjustments made within the communications system.

Institutionalization of the Media. Although the press was already big business early in the twentieth century, the interlocking media have become even more so since the advent of television and the general information explosion. In response to the ever growing demand for information, and the profits that accrue in satisfying the demand, the news system has become a mass institution that meshes with government, business, and other institutions. It must meet daily deadlines for complex production and diffusion of news; to do so it has developed a bureauracy of specialists, most of whom are unionized.

In journalism of all forms there are at least 600,000 employees, of whom perhaps one-tenth are engaged in the actual gathering, writing, and editing of news. The communications industry as a whole encompasses a huge sector of the American economy and some of the largest and most powerful institutions.

In the struggle to stay profitably competitive in the face of rising costs, higher taxes, and increasing union demands, the media have been moving toward consolidation in corporate chains and diversified conglomerates. While such collectivism has economic advantages, it also militates toward standardization, a condition once shunned in journalism.

The transformation of the media since World War II has inevitably brought a change in the way in which news is regarded and treated. Except in some small communities, personal journalism has been replaced by corporate journalism based increasingly on the market philosophy. The effect is reflected in such basic journalistic concerns as the definition of legitimate news, the adversary aspect of newsgathering, the diversity of information and opinion offered, and the amount of entertainment and advertising included.

NOTES

1. John Tebbel, *The Media in America* (New York: Thomas Y. Crowell Company, 1974), p. 181.

SUGGESTED READING

Barnouw, Erik. *Tube of Plenty*. New York: Oxford University Press, 1975.

Mott, Frank Luther. *American Journalism*. Rev. ed. New York: Macmillan, 1967.

Tebbel, John. *The Media in America*. New York: Thomas Y. Crowell Company, 1974.

4

The Media Organizations

There is a tendency to think of "the press" in the United States as a monolithic entity; in fact, it is probably more diverse and complex than the press of any other country. The American news system is made up of thousands of large and small newspapers and broadcast stations under private ownership. As commercial businesses, the newspapers and stations operate, in the main, independently from one another. Conforming to a historical pattern based on political and economic factors, they are still largely oriented to the local community, although this pattern has begun to change with the industry's recent trend toward centralization.

If the newspapers and broadcast stations are the body of the industry, the press associations (or wire services) are the backbone. Through a branching network of communications, these associations supply the local papers and stations with news from around the world. Also contributing to the general mass of reportage and opinion are feature syndicates, magazine and book publishers, newsletter publishers, and advertising and public relations agencies. While all of the media are parts of a vast interlocking communications system, each plays its own role in the competitive marketplace of information and ideas; each has its own structure and appeal.

Local Orientation. The starting point for understanding the overall structure of the American news system is recognition of its localized commercial character. This quality influences the content and ownership of the media that are the primary sources of daily news—newspapers and broadcast stations—and prescribes their market and operating reach.

There are no "national" daily newspapers distributed extensively throughout the country. The *New York Times* comes closest to this description; but while it enjoys high prestige and is read by influential people, its circulation is primarily in the New York area and its national readership is limited. The *Wall Street Journal* and the *Christian Science Monitor* have nationwide distribution, but the *Journal* is a specialized business paper and the *Monitor* has a relatively small circulation. The broadcast networks and their affiliated stations interconnect nationally, but their systems operate through local outlets with limited audience ranges. Thus, as Ben H. Bagdikian points out in *The Information Machines*, "the typical American consumer receives all his daily printed and broadcast news from a local private enterprise."[1]

In this respect, the United States differs from most other countries, where principal newspapers are printed in urban centers and distributed nationally, and broadcasting typically is centralized in a government-controlled monopoly. (In Britain, for example, a half-dozen dailies printed in London are sold throughout the country and represent nearly three-quarters of the national circulation.)

Political and Economic Factors. In an analysis of the American news system, Bagdikian cites two fundamental reasons for the longstanding local orientation:[2]

First, unlike most other countries, the United States has a political structure that focuses on local, rather than national, control of a wide variety of government functions that directly affect daily life: schools, property taxes, land use, public health, business regulation. These functions are controlled separately by approximately 35,000 municipalities and townships throughout the country. To keep all citizens continually informed about the day-to-day activities in their local communities would be impossible for a national medium.

Second, the American media have always been carriers of merchandising information and dependent on advertising for operating revenue. The United States economy is heavily consumer-oriented, and Americans do most of their buying locally. Therefore, the bulk of the advertising in the media has been local, reinforcing the local character of the newspapers and broadcast stations.

Bagdikian points to signs of a widening of the local focus. Experience has shown that the economic factor tends to outweigh the political factor with the media; as commercial enterprises, the media adjust to merchandising markets rather than to civic boundaries. And the merchandising function, Bagdikian notes, continues to favor ever larger geographical territories, "so that the cost of reaching each consumer will drop." Thus, as merchandising markets expand into the suburbs and standardized advertising becomes feasible for larger areas, the media extend across civic boundaries. In the process, their neighborhood or community roots weaken.

These factors underlie the movement toward local media monopolies and corporate media chains that are increasing the control of national and regional organizations over local outlets. In many cases, these larger media organizations are controlled, in turn, by industrial conglomerates whose principal interests are outside the communications field.

NEWSPAPERS

Despite the impact of television, newspapers remain the heart of the news business. They are the basic source of most of the daily information and opinion distributed to the American public. Newspapers and the news wire services, which feed each other in an interrelated news net, produce the bulk of original reporting; broadcast news is primarily a "headline service." Whether large or small, the approximately 1,750 daily newspapers and 8,800 weeklies continue to be the principal voices and monitors of their communities. About 61 million copies of daily newspapers are sold every day.

Growth and Change. The failure of some metropolitan dailies in recent years has led to an erroneous impression that newspapers are a dying industry. In fact, newspaper publishing is among the top ten growth industries in the United States, and rates high in such business factors as employment and value of shipping. Newspapers claim a larger share of advertising, in terms of dollars spent, than any other medium, and most newspapers continue to be highly profitable.

Since World War II, as population has increased, total circulation of daily newspapers has risen more than 20 percent. The average number of pages in dailies has doubled (with most of the increase going to advertising). And despite a trend toward consolidation, the total number of both dailies and weeklies has remained relatively stable over the same period.

Daily newspapers constitute the main body of the industry, at least from the business standpoint. They have approximately 90 percent of the circulation, manpower, and revenues. While the large metropolitan dailies are the most visible and represent half of the nation's daily circulation, they are not typical of the industry in terms of numbers. More than half the daily newspapers are published in communities with less than 25,000 population, and nearly half have circulations of 10,000 or less.

Regardless of their size, however, newspapers have similar organizations, operating procedures, and types of audiences. Size is not necessarily an indicator of either excellence or profitability; some of the best edited and most prosperous have small circulations. Moreover, many small weeklies command closer attention and exert greater social and political influence on their readers' lives than do large dailies from nearby cities.

Newspaper publishing has undergone some major adjustments in recent years, partly because of changes in living patterns, partly because of competition from television. Many papers in large cities and small towns have been forced to close, but new papers have been started in the new booming suburbs. Most newspapers have became monopolies in their communities, and independent ownership has been giving way to corporate "chain" ownership. New approaches to content have been introduced. And after decades without change in production methods, the industry is becoming automated.

The Dailies. Daily newspapers had their greatest growth during the westward population expansion in the second half of the nineteenth century, reaching a peak number of 2,461 in 1916. However, many of the papers started in new cities were economically weak and fell by the wayside with World War I. The total number declined in succeeding years until it stabilized near 1,750. Since World War II, total circulation of dailies has generally kept pace with the rate of population gain.

	Number of Dailies	Total circulation of all dailies
1945	1,749	48,383,000
1955	1,760	56,147,000
1965	1,751	60,358,000
1975	1,756	60,655,431

Source: *Editor and Publisher*

Half the nation's daily circulation in 1975 was generated by 118 papers with circulations of 100,000 or more; these were the big-city papers whose prestige and newsgathering resources made them a strong political and social force. Among the circulation leaders were the *New York Daily News* (2.1 million), the *Los Angeles Times* (1 million), and the *New York Times* (803,000). The *Wall Street Journal* sold a million copies a day in six regional editions, but it is a specialty paper devoted primarily to business and financial news. The average urban reader had access to a daily with a median circulation of roughly 400,000.

At the same time, the largest single category in terms of number of newspapers, 518, was the group with circulations of 10,000 to 25,000. In almost all cases, these were the sole paper in their communities and the primary source of local and state news.

Afternoon dailies outnumbered morning dailies by more than four to one. This situation grew out of the days when the largely blue-collar work force left home early in the morning and returned home with plenty of time to read the afternoon paper before dinner (that was before the evening TV newscast became a competitor). But while the morning papers represented less than 23 percent of all dailies in the mid-1970s, they had 42 percent of the total circulation. The reason was that some of the largest-circulation and most prestigious metropolitan dailies were morning papers: for example, the *Times* and *Daily News* in New York, the *Los Angeles Times*, and the *Washington Post*.

A consensus likely would designate the *New York Times* and the *Washington Post* as the best newspapers in the country, or at least the most influential nationally. While they are seldom seen by most Americans, they are read regularly and thoroughly by government officials, diplomats, business leaders, educators, and people who, on the air or in print, provide the national news. The *Times* and the *Post* are filed in most libraries, and more than half the newspaper and magazine items quoted in the *Congressional Record* by legislators come from the two papers.

The Weeklies. Published once a week (or in some cases, semi-weekly), these community newspapers range in their bases from the small rural towns to neighborhoods in large cities to the wealthy old suburbs to the new suburbs of young households. Most circulations are 1,000 to 2,000, although some reach up to 15,000, even higher in some suburbs.

	1955	1965	1975
Number of weeklies	9,126	8,989	8,824
Number of semiweeklies	324	357	506

Source: Statistical Abstract of the United States

While the total number of these papers has remained about the same, their total circulation has climbed steadily since 1960 as a result of national population growth and changing community patterns. Subscribers represent nearly half of all American households. In most of these households, except in remote rural towns, the weekly is a second newspaper bought in addition to a daily.

The community weekly traditionally has been run by a local entrepreneur, although the trend in recent years, as with dailies, has been toward consolidation into group ownership. The community paper has been called the last stronghold of free individual expression in a society that seems to become every day more "impersonal." This is perhaps the main reason that such

papers thrive in neighborhoods of metropolitan center cities
such as New York, Chicago, and Philadelphia.

The weekly paper usually is an integral part of the community or neighborhood—an extension of the community bulletin board. It provides leadership and a rallying point for
community activities. Its substance is strictly local news and
issues that involve the readers and directly affect their lives. Its
advertising, mostly local, receives close reader attention and is
a key factor in the local economy. For these reasons, the weekly
newspaper generally is read carefully and thoroughly, and often
is held as a reference, by all members of a household. The result
is that most weeklies have a strong cultural impact despite their
small size.

Specials. There are several categories of newspapers that fall
outside the definition of the conventional daily or weekly. They
are aimed at special-interest groups, or serve a specific purpose
outside the scope of standard news, or are produced by college
students. Most are published weekly.

ALTERNATIVE NEWSPAPERS. These flourished in the 1960s and
their common denominator was ideology. Their founders said
that they were communicating with segments of the population
—mostly the liberal and intellectual young adults—who were
disenchanted with American society and the conventional press.
While the more successful papers dealt competently with social
and political ills, many of the smaller papers concentrated on
such subjects as the antiwar movement, hippies, the drug culture,
unconventional lifestyles, and bizarre religions. By the mid-1970s,
when the Vietnam War was over and the general unrest had
subsided, only a few papers like the *Village Voice*, the *Bay
Guardian, Rolling Stone*, and the *Boston Phoenix* retained much
impact; most of the smaller "underground" papers had faded.

BLACK NEWSPAPERS. These cover news of particular interest to
black people. In 1975 there were 298 such papers in 38 states,
mostly in large cities, with a combined circulation of about 4
million. More than a third of the total were concentrated in
California, Illinois, New York, and Texas.

PROFESSIONAL NEWSPAPERS. There are about 100 of these, and
each covers news only in a specific field: agriculture, apparel,
engineering, entertainment, legal and commercial, real estate,
sports. These papers are read avidly by people in the respective

fields, and occasionally they provide tips for stories in the dailies.

COLLEGE NEWSPAPERS. Most campuses have newspapers produced by students. The majority are prepared for campus consumption, but the larger papers rival the local community newspaper for general readership. They carry national and international news from the wire services, and cover municipal and local news regularly. Among the larger student papers are the *Daily Texan* of the University of Texas, with a circulation of close to 40,000, the *Minnesota Daily* of the University of Minnesota with 35,000, and the *Daily Californian* of the University of California at Berkeley with 30,000.

Organization. All newspapers have a common organization with five basic divisions:

1. *Editorial* gathers and prepares the news, opinion materials, entertainment, and other information that is not advertising.

2. *Advertising* solicits and prepares the display and classified ads.

3. *Production* transforms the editorial and advertising materials into type and graphics and prints the newspaper.

4. *Circulation* sells and distributes the papers.

5. *Business* oversees the commercial transactions.

Employees. The number of newspaper employees varies widely, from the more than 6,000 at the *New York Times* to 10 or fewer on a small daily or weekly. An average-size paper with 35,000 circulation employs about 200 persons. The industrial operations claim the majority of a paper's manpower, energies, and revenues, with more than half the employees engaged in mechanical production and distribution. The personnel who actually gather and prepare the news—the editorial department—represent only about a fifth of the average newspaper's total staff.

Changing Patterns. Newspaper patterns began to change in the 1950s with the expansion of the interstate highway system, the resultant growth of suburbs, and the maturing of television news. These developments affected newspaper circulation logistics, advertising markets, and news-reading habits during a period of steady increase in newspaper production costs. The net impact was the addition of papers in the new communities, where capital tended to flow, and survival of the fittest in the old communities.

Thus, while the total number of newspapers has remained

about the same over the years, the alignment has changed. In 1975, for example, 13 dailies suspended publication or merged with other papers, but 13 new dailies were started.

Between 1961 and 1970, according to a report of the Newspaper Survival Study, a research project funded by the Markle Foundation, 164 daily newspapers failed and 170 new ones were launched. While most of the failed papers were small and typically new enterprises, the major significance in the statistics is that the list included some of the nation's oldest and best-known metropolitan giants. Since 1960, cities that have lost newspapers include New York, Washington, Chicago, Los Angeles, Boston, San Francisco, Detroit, Houston, Newark, Hartford, and Cleveland. New York, which once boasted fourteen dailies, went from eight just after World War II to three. Among the respected victims were the *Herald Tribune*, the *World Telegram and Sun*, and the *Journal American*.

Big-City Problems. The effect of the converging demographic and economic forces is most evident in the big cities. The reality for metropolitan newspapers is that their most loyal readers are vanishing. While 75 percent of the nation's population now lives in large urban areas, there has been an increasing flow to the suburbs of middle-class whites, replaced in the central cities by lower-class blacks and Hispanics, who are less interested in newspapers. By the mid-1970s, the suburbs had about 56 percent of the people living in the metropolitan areas. Whereas the metropolitan newspaper's audience for both news and advertising once was concentrated in the city near the newspaper production plant, it is now dispersed to the fringes.

This change means that city papers have to be hauled longer distances, usually through heavy traffic if the paper comes out in the afternoon. Thus, delivery is slower and more costly. The demographic change also means that more people, the suburbanites, do their shopping mainly outside the city, a fact which affects newspaper advertising; and suburbanites develop new civic loyalties and interests, which affect their reading preferences. Large numbers of suburbanites have turned to the new suburban papers for local news of their new home communities, and rely on television for national and international news.

All this has come during a time of increasing costs for labor, newsprint, gasoline for delivery trucks, utilities, taxes, and other operating necessities. In a highly competitive business, the combination of higher costs and the loss of circulation and advertising proved economically unfeasible for the papers that folded.

Monopolies. As a result of the deaths and mergers, most Americans no longer have a choice in the local printed news available to them: 97.5 percent of the nation's daily newspapers are now monopolies in their communities. Head-to-head competition between newspapers has been virtually eliminated. Such competition had long been considered vital to the press's role because it prodded newspapers to keep an eye on their rivals and on the public interest as they saw it. With competition, diversity of news and opinion offered to the public was the rule; without competition, diversity is the exception today.

A half-century ago there were 700 cities in the United States with competing newspapers; today there are fewer than 50 out of the 1,500 cities with daily newspapers. Only New York has more than two competing managements and since Chicago lost the *Daily News* in March, 1978, New York and Philadelphia are the only large cities with at least three newspapers.

Chains. Historically, newspapers have tended to have local ownership, usually a private family or closed corporation with deep roots and interests in the community. This tradition grew out of the newspaper's orientation to local news. Some of the country's most important newspapers are still family-owned, the management handed down from generation to generation; but the trend, as the costs and complexities of newspapering have mounted, has been toward corporate ownership. The reasons are economic.

Because the surviving monopoly newspapers have no competition for readers and markets, they are highly profitable and attractive as businesses. This is especially true in small to medium-sized cities where the papers are largely free of big-city economic burdens. New technology has improved the production of most, and advertising, which provides the average newspaper with roughly 80 percent of its revenues, has remained strong.

The result is that corporate newspaper groups, or chains, have become increasingly interested in adding newspapers as investment properties, and have bought up independent operations at prices too good for most local managements to resist. Two factors have eased the way: first, tax laws are such that newspapers can save on taxes through investment in other papers; second, there has been a trend toward independent owners selling their stock to the public as one way of avoiding heavy inheritance taxes.

Thus, 49 daily newspapers changed hands in 1975, and 72 were transferred the following year, most at high prices. For example, Capital Cities Communications, owner of four small papers, thirteen broadcast stations, and *Women's Wear Daily*, purchased the Kansas City Star Company, publisher of the evening *Star* and the morning *Times*, for $125 million, said to be twice the book value of the company. Rupert Murdoch, an Australian publisher, paid more than $30 million for the *New York Post*.

Newspaper chains are not new, but they have expanded immensely in recent years in line with the general corporate consolidation in the American economy. By the mid-1970s, 60 percent of the nation's newspapers, with 71 percent of the total daily circulation, were controlled by 168 corporate owners. The top 25 chains controlled 52 percent of the circulation.

Leading in number of papers owned at the beginning of 1977 were Gannett with 73, Thomson with 57, and Knight-Ridder with 34. Leaders in terms of daily circulation were Knight-Ridder with 3,725,000 and Newhouse (30 papers) with 3,350,000.

The concentration process has even led to chains buying chains. In 1976 four big chains bought six smaller ones. The most notable was Newhouse's purchase of Booth Newspapers' eight dailies in Michigan and the Sunday supplement *Parade* for more than $300 million, believed to be the biggest newspaper sale in history.

Newspapers are also becoming parts of conglomerates, the collection of different kinds of companies in one corporation. A conglomerate might own broadcast stations, magazines, book publishing houses, manufacturing companies, record firms, car rental agencies, and even a baseball team, as well as newspapers. Such arrangements raise questions about possible conflicts of interest, and about the priority given to a news operation by the business-minded corporate leadership.

Newspaper Audience. Newspapers reach all but the very young. Studies have shown that about 90 percent of adult Americans regularly see a daily newspaper, and most of the rest read a weekly. The most avid readers of newspapers have these common characteristics: they are well educated, in white-collar jobs, married and between the ages of 30 and 54, relatively affluent, and residents of metropolitan areas. These people tend to be homeowners, with roots and a stake in their communities. Adults do more newspaper reading than young people; and older people use the paper mainly for information and views of public affairs while young people are likely to use it more for entertainment.

In comparing newspapers and the broadcast media as sources of news, readers generally cite the following as advantages of newspapers: Newspapers provide details, background, interpretation, and opinion, whereas television and radio usually provide only the headlines. Newspapers can be carried around and read at leisure or when convenient, whereas television and radio are anchored to one place and news programs are available only at specific times. Newspapers can be held for reference, whereas broadcast news cannot.

Nevertheless, some studies indicate that a growing number of people prefer television over newspapers as their primary source of news. Most frequently cited are the periodic polls taken since 1959 by the Roper Organization for the Television Information Office.

The key question in the polls is: "I'd like to ask you where you usually get most of your news about what's going on in the world today—from the newspapers or radio or television or magazines or talking with people, or where?" In 1959 the proportion of respondents who mentioned television was 51 percent; in 1976, the figure was 64 percent. The proportion who cited newspapers in 1959 was 57 percent, and in 1976 it was under 20 percent (some people named more than one "primary" source).

Some newspaper advocates have criticized the Roper question as being "ambiguous," and contend that poll results can be influenced by the way the survey is designed and the questions are asked. They have pointed to other studies in which newspapers have fared better.

Opinion Research Corporation, for example, asked a national probability sample of 2,023 adults: "Suppose there is some news you are very much interested in. Where would you be most likely to find out all there is about it?" Newspapers were cited by 50 percent of the respondents, television by 46 percent, radio by 12 percent, and magazines by 11 percent (some people mentioned more than one source). A 1977 national survey for the Newspaper Readership Council, an organization of newspaper organizations, found that 69 percent of those interviewed read newspapers as a source of news on any given day, 62 percent watched TV newscasts daily, 49 percent listened to radio news, and 25 percent used all three news sources.

What is clear, despite the conflicting studies, is that neither print nor broadcast is likely to push the other out of the news business. Broadcast generally is associated with national and international news and fast-breaking dramatic events such as riots, earthquakes, and election returns. Newspapers emphasize local news, and go beyond the mere presentation of news to illumination and interpretation. So the two media seem to reinforce each other, with the result that most people use both.

Long-Term Concerns. Despite their continued prosperity, many newspaper executives in the 1970s found reasons for concern about their industry's future. Readership was showing signs of eroding, and though newspapers still were the dominant advertising medium, television had claimed an increasing share since 1960. The long-term trend was downward for daily newspapers sold per American household. Many families that once bought two newspapers were now buying only one.

Many explanations, aside from television, were suggested for the trend. Studies showed a marked drop among the young, many of whom contended that newspapers were dull, impersonal, and repetitive. An American Newspaper Publishers Association Study in 1977 found that people from twenty-one to thirty-four years old considered television more accurate, informative, ethical, easier to use, more relaxing, and more necessary than newspapers. Other explanations offered: People were marrying and settling into their own homes and communities at a later age and thus were less interested in the local news—about schools, property taxes, community politics—emphasized by newspapers. The rising cost of living and increasing competition for people's time, including leisure activities and specialized magazines, worked against purchase of newspapers. Some regional newspapers, to reduce operating costs, cut off distribution to readers in outlying areas.

Content Changes. Whatever the reason for lagging circulation, many newspaper executives, traditionally resistant to analysis of their operations, sought new answers and approaches. There was flurry of experimentation in newspaper content and format in the 1970s. Changes included larger photographs, use of color, wider columns, more attractive typefaces, and subject labels to make stories easier to find. Some papers added news summaries, more featurized local news and sports, pages devoted to home-living, leisure activities, and how-to columns by experts about personal interests. Several large papers started separate sections with news and features directed at specific suburban readers.

Automation. One of the last major industries to become automated, newspapers began making up for lost decades. Since 1960, most major dailies—and many smaller ones—have computerized all, or at least some, of their operations. The video display terminal (VDT) has replaced the typewriter in the newsroom, computer data banks have replaced newspaper clippings "morgues," and automatic typesetting equipment has replaced manual operations in the composing room. This automation has eliminated costly, time-consuming steps and has increased productivity. One newspaper, for example, saved more than $1 million a year by reducing from four hours to 90 seconds the time needed for setting type for a page of classified ads.

PRESS ASSOCIATIONS

The press associations are wholesalers of news on a global scale. They do not publish or broadcast information directly to the consumer; rather, in a strangely anonymous fashion, they provide the other media with news reports, and by-products of the news such as pictures and features, that are beyond the reach of local reporting staffs. For their services, the press associations, and the supplementary syndicates, charge fees that are scaled in accordance with the purchaser's circulation and the amount of editorial material provided.

The press associations, also known as wire services or news agencies, provide the bulk of the foreign and national news disseminated by the American media. Even the largest news-papers, with their own reporters in Washington and abroad, rely heavily on wire-service dispatches to achieve a well-balanced news presentation.

AP and UPI. The two American-owned wire services, the Associated Press (AP) and United Press International (UPI), are the largest and most competitive. Each has about 2,500 clients. Between them they service virtually every American daily news-paper, the television and radio networks and most of the stations, the newsmagazines, some government agencies, and even private businesses and organizations that have a news service require-ment. Many of the larger newspapers and stations use both services. AP and UPI also are major suppliers of news to foreign media, making the American agencies a vital element in inter-national communications. Both agencies are headquartered in New York City and have bureaus throughout the world.

The Associated Press, the older of the two agencies, is a non-profit cooperative newsgathering organization. Media that use its service are members of the cooperative, participate in its operations, and pay assessments to cover costs. Unlike the AP, United Press International is not a cooperative; it is a privately owned company, controlled by the Scripps-Howard newspaper interests. It sells its newsgathering service on a contract basis (at rates comparable to AP assessments) to "clients" or "sub-scribers."

Newsgathering. The press associations' system for obtaining news essentially is an extension of the local newspaper system. It includes two basic news channels.

First, the associations maintain bureaus in major cities, and their own reporters cover the news directly. In smaller cities, the coverage is handled by part-time correspondents ("stringers") who usually are employees of the local newspaper or broadcast station.

Second, the wire services have access, either directly or in-directly, to the news gathered by local outlets which they service. Under the rules of the AP, every member of the cooperative must make its stories available for distribution to other members. For example, a reporter for a Pittsburgh newspaper covers a story for potential use by all AP members as well as his own paper. Although the UPI does not have a formal sharing arrangement like the AP's, the agency's local stringers usually have ready access to stories covered by their newspapers or broadcast stations.

Because wire service members or clients are everywhere, and their readers and listeners have varying interests, stories selected for wire service distribution have wide, general appeal. They are likely to originate in national or state capitols rather than city halls, and deal with big events rather than small local events. The stories are written objectively ("down the middle") because they must meet the standards of thousands of editors representing all shades of political persuasion, social conscious-ness, and religious beliefs. The daily report of a wire service is a "cafeteria of news" from which local editors can choose stories for their own use.

The bread-and-butter fare continues to be news events as they happen, but in recent years there has been a new emphasis on stories that try to get behind the news—in-depth explorations of such subjects as the environment, consumerism, and infla-tion. The shift is in line with the shift in needs by the press associations' customers.

Transmission. To assemble the news and deliver it to members or clients, AP and UPI maintain networks of leased telegraph circuits in the United States and leased cable and teleprinter radio circuits overseas. News stories are transmitted from wire service bureaus over the circuits to teleprinter machines in news-paper and broadcast station offices. The teleprinter machines type out the stories on continuous rolls of paper.

The transmission process has been speeded up dramatically by the computerization of machinery and the introduction of high-speed printers. Whereas the old teletype speed was 66 words a minute for normal news copy, it is now up to 1,200 words a minute; and for stock-market tables, the rate is 12,000 words a minute. This technology enables the Associated Press, for example, to transmit an overall total of 3 million words a day.

The system revolves around a main trunk, or transcontinental, circuit controlled by the press association's headquarters in New York. This trunk carries the major stories of the day. Branching off the main trunk are regional and state wires, controlled by key bureaus that serve as relay points. These secondary wires carry additional, more localized stories of interest to communities covered by the wires. The relay bureaus also channel local stories that are considered of national appeal.

In addition to the general news wires, the press associations have separate circuits for sports and financial news that serve mainly the large metropolitan newspapers and stations; and radio news wires with stories written in a format and language for easy delivery on the air. The agencies also provide telegraphic photo service, special features, columns, and other supplementary material.

The interlocking system is designed to give each customer a balanced news report with information relevant to the customer's needs. Every customer usually receives the big story out of Washington, and likewise a story originating in a small bureau if the material is regarded as universally interesting or significant by relaying editors along the circuits. On the other hand, a story of special interest only in Maine is not likely to be relayed to customers in Montana, and vice versa.

Press associations operate under intense time pressures. Because their service is subject to different time zones, there is a deadline every minute—for some members or clients somewhere. Therefore, wire services must constantly "keep on top" of stories, feeding the latest developments into the circuits so that customers can have up-to-the-minute news when they go to press or on the air. This condition accounts for the traditional competition between the wire services to be "first with the news."

Foreign Wire Services. The only foreign press association that rivals AP and UPI worldwide is Reuters, the British service. Compared with AP and UPI, Reuters has relatively few outlets in the United States; but its outlets include many of the major newspapers and the broadcast networks that purchase the service primarily because of the good foreign coverage. The French wire service Agence France-Press, which is strong in French-speaking countries, also has some outlets in the United States.

Most other countries have national news services that have exchange agreements with the major press associations, creating a global communications chain.

Dissemination of information from areas under Communist control is dominated by Tass, the Soviet agency, and Hsinhua, the Chinese agency. Though both services are government-controlled monopolies, serving as propaganda outlets for their governments, they nevertheless are primary sources of news about the Soviet Union and China and often about other Communist-controlled nations as well. In these nations, coverage by Western news organizations is restricted.

Syndicates. Several major newspapers have established syndicates of their own and sell their services to other papers. Leaders in the field are the *New York Times* (over 400 subscribers in 1977), the *Los Angeles Times–Washington Post* partnership, and the Copley News Service. These syndicates generally do not try to compete with AP and UPI on "spot" news developments; rather, they provide supplementary background, interpretive, and feature material. By purchasing syndicate services, smaller papers are able to enlarge their scope and publish the writings of prominent correspondents and columnists of the more prestigious papers.

Another kind of news service has emerged with the growing number of newspaper chains. Members of the chains are linked by wire for exchange of news stories and other material within their groups.

Feature syndicates, which are distinct from the regular news services, are a major source of editorial material. They provide features ranging from comics and how-to articles to "canned" editorials and columns about politics and religion. There are more than 100 such syndicates, but about a dozen of the bigger ones provide the bulk of the features used in the American media. Sales competition among the syndicates is strong; although some of the established features remain popular year after year, dozens of new ones are introduced into the market annually. The usual arrangement is that a syndicate grants a newspaper the exclusive right to a particular feature in a given geographic area.

BROADCASTING

Radio and television are truly mass media, reaching huge audiences on a national scale. As communicators of information to the public, the broadcast media differ from newspapers in two basic respects: First, because radio and television use public airwaves, they are regulated by the government through the Federal Communications Commission (FCC). Second, because their essential mission is merchandising and they are financed by advertising, commercial radio and television give overwhelming priority to entertainment that attracts the widest possible audiences.

In comparison with entertainment, news and public affairs programs receive relatively minor attention and air time. As a result, broadcast news is essentially a summary or headline service that tends to follow the lead of printed news.

Public, or noncommercial, broadcasting tries to fill the gaps in public affairs as well as culture and education, but suffers chronically from a shortage of funds. Cable television has enormous potential as the basis of a "wired nation," but has been slow to develop for a variety of economic and regulatory reasons.

Mass Media. Of all the media, the broadcast networks come closest to being national news organs on a daily basis. Through simultaneous transmission over hundreds of stations scattered across the country, the networks can reach millions of people with the same news at the same time. And broadcasting has the appeal to attract large audiences because its sound and sight characteristics create a sense of immediacy and vicarious participation.

It was estimated, for example, that 78 million Americans watched President Carter on three television networks in December 1977, when, in an interview with reporters, he talked about his first year in office. The number of viewers seeing and hearing the President firsthand was approximately 17 million more than the number of daily newspapers distributed the following day with secondhand reports of the interview. In a lighter vein, mixing entertainment with sports reportage, the 1978 Super Bowl football game was watched by an estimated 85 million people.

In the average American home, according to A. C. Nielsen surveys, the TV set is on nearly seven hours a day; and during prime evening hours (8 P.M. to 11 P.M.), the most popular viewing period, television is watched in 64 percent of all homes by an average of two persons per set. Radio claims less time per household per day, but it is said to reach more people for some part of every day.

The audience for both radio and television is nearly universal, but studies show that blue-collar, less-educated people spend more time with broadcasting than do better-educated, economically advanced people. One advantage that both radio and television have over newspapers is that they do not require literacy and can be enjoyed by very young children. A big plus for radio is that listeners can do other things while listening, including driving a car.

Despite their capability to reach mass audiences, the broadcast media have never been used extensively as news channels. Because of their commercial nature, radio and television are marketing and entertainment instruments that include news only as a necessary by-product.

A Commercial System. Although educational and other noncommercial stations share the airwaves, broadcasting in the United States is largely run by profitmaking enterprises. The overwhelming majority of the 7,800 radio stations and 950 television stations are commercial. Most stations are affiliated with national networks, although national programming is more prevalent in television than in radio.

Radio and television have grown steadily since their inceptions, but the number of stations is restricted because the number of transmission channels, or airwave frequencies, is physically limited. This limitation promotes profitability in broadcasting, inasmuch as there is an ever expanding demand by advertisers

GROWTH OF BROADCAST SERVICE

| | Commercial Radio | | Noncommercial Radio |
	AM stations	FM stations	FM stations
1955	2,669	552	122
1965	4,012	1,270	255
1975	5,434	2,648	725

| | Commercial TV | | Noncommercial TV | |
	VHF	UHF	VHF	UHF
1955	294	117	9	—
1965	487	99	54	34
1975	513	198	95	147

Source: *Broadcasting Yearbook*

for a finite amount of air time. In 1976, the before-tax profits for all of commercial broadcasting topped $1 billion for the first time, and network profits alone totaled nearly $300 million.

Because broadcasting, especially television, is profitable, there is steady competition for ownership of stations as investments. Every year dozens of stations change hands. While a license to operate a station in the mid-1970s cost only $150, the average market value of a television station in the top 50 markets was about $20 million.

The profit motive is the basis for commercial broadcasting's concentration on entertainment. Radio and television operations are financed by advertising; and advertisers, seeking to promote their products as widely as possible, want the mass audiences that are attracted regularly by entertainment. Audience surveys show that entertainment programs consistently outdraw news and public affairs programs, except for some special events such as a presidential speech or a space shot.

The larger the audience, the higher is the cost to advertisers for air time. This accounts for the fierce competition for program ratings. One rating point for a national network program means approximately a million TV households listening in, and an extra point translates into added millions of dollars in net profits a year.

Government Regulation. The rationale for FCC regulation of broadcasting is that, since the airwaves are limited and in the public domain, they should be entrusted to users with a sense of public responsibility. The regulations affect broadcast stations as to geographic distribution, ownership, and, in minor respects, programming. Stations are licensed by the government and, under FCC rules, must "serve the public interest, convenience and necessity." The commission does not license networks, because networks do not use the airwaves; they use privately leased lines to relay programs to broadcasting stations.

The location, frequency band, and power of stations are determined by the FCC. A major consideration is avoidance of interference with other stations. Other considerations are market demand and the desire for equitable geographic distribution.

In the mid-1970s, the distribution of commercial stations was as follows: for radio, 4,434 AM (amplitude modulation) and 2,648 FM (frequency modulation) stations were dispersed among some 2,700 communities; for television, 513 VHF (very high frequency) and 198 UHF (ultra-high frequency) stations were located in 285 metropolitan areas.

Because of the limitation factors, the largest number of radio stations in a single area was 34, and the maximum number of VHF television stations in one area was seven. Of the communities with stations, the majority had only one station, but in most places signals could be received from stations in nearby communities. To avoid interference with each other, stations using the same channel must be at least 170 miles apart.

To promote diversification and minimize concentration of control of the broadcast media, the FCC imposes the following restrictions: no person or group can operate more than one station of the same service (AM, FM, or TV) in the same community; no single entity can own more than seven stations in each service anywhere in the nation, and in television no more than five of the stations can be VHF; no owner of three VHF stations in the top 50 markets can purchase other VHF's in the top 50 markets; newspaper owners cannot purchase broadcast properties in the same community. Moreover, there was movement in the 1970s, through court action, to break up 160 existing cross-ownerships of newspaper-television and newspaper-radio combinations.

Programming, advertising, and station management are the primary responsibility of broadcast licensees; the FCC does not monitor these practices on a day-to-day basis. The commission does, however, review performance when a station's license is up for renewal. Although the commission does not prescribe how much time should be devoted to news and public affairs, it requires a licensee to show, with program logs, that the station is meeting the community's social and cultural needs and interests. The generally accepted measure of the public-service function is 1 percent news and 5 percent public-service programming. Examples of a public-service program are a panel discussion about a proposed school budget, a film about local environmental problems, or a broadcast of a church service.

The FCC's performance review is nominal at best, for several reasons. One is that a community's needs and interests can be interpreted in many ways, and they are likely to differ in different communities. Another is the difficulty of defining what con-

stitutes public affairs in terms of community activities, education, religion, culture. A third is that about 2,500 licenses come
up for renewal every year, and analyzing representative weekly
logs from that many stations is an almost impossible task for
a small FCC staff. Nevertheless, the FCC, with its power to
revoke a license, serves as a reminder for stations to stay in line.

Broadcasting is not a common carrier operation; therefore,
broadcasters are not required to sell or give time to all who seek
to go on the air. Thus, public access is severely limited; in
effect, broadcasting's management determines what is put on
radio and TV. The FCC's Fairness Doctrine stipulates, however,
that when a station presents one viewpoint on a controversial
public issue, the public interest requires that there be reasonable
opportunity for presentation of opposing viewpoints. The
"equal-time" principle also applies to political candidates.

Networking. Although public policy calls for allocation of
broadcasting facilities on a local basis, and most stations are
locally owned, commercial radio and television operate in systems that are essentially national. The stations are interconnected electronically in affiliation with national networks that
produce and distribute, through the local stations, standardized
programming and advertising under central control. Networking is the dominant pattern in television, and it prevails in a
large share of radio programming.

The networking pattern traces back to the beginnings of radio.
With newspapers oriented to the local community, and in firm
control of local advertising, radio had to offer something different to compete successfully. With technology available for inter-
connection, radio's answer was programming and advertising
for a national audience.

Standardized programming, distributed from centrally controlled studios by "a flip of a switch," meant economies of size
that enabled local stations to have entertainment and news that
they could not afford on their own. Popular programs such as
Amos n' Andy and H. V. Kaltenborn's news commentaries
captured large audiences that appealed to national advertising.
And since the cost of producing a program in New York was
fixed, the profits grew with the number of stations that shared
in the distribution of the program.

The programming and advertising fed each other, and soon

shaped radio into a national medium. When television came along, it followed the same networking pattern for the same reasons. Television grew rapidly and eventually overshadowed radio.

Today there are four basic radio networks: ABC (which divides its operations into three AM networks and one FM network), CBS, NBC, and Mutual. Under FCC rules, they are allowed outright ownership of only a few local stations, but each network has affiliations and contracts with other stations.

There are three major television networks: ABC, CBS, and NBC. Each owns five local stations outright and has approximately 200 affiliated stations. About 100 TV stations operate as independents. Network-affiliated stations claim almost all of the audience in the country's top 50 markets, where three-fourths of Americans live.

In networking, local affiliates contract with the networks to carry centrally controlled programs, with mutual benefits from advertising. By law, an affiliate has the right to reject any network program. The contract normally is for two years, and there is nothing to stop a station from jumping to another network if it thinks the switch will bring larger audiences and more money. By the same token, a network's ratings—and advertising income—are affected by the number of affiliates it has as outlets for the network programs and by the quality of the station's signals.

Networking is particularly pronounced in television: about 85 percent of all TV programming is centrally controlled, the rest produced locally. During the prime evening viewing period, network programming amounts to approximately 95 percent. In radio, on the other hand, less than half the programming is network-controlled. With television claiming the bulk of national advertising and revenues in broadcasting, most radio stations have bolstered their coffers and schedules with local advertising and local programs—primarily music, talk shows, headline news, and special-interest subjects.

The networking system and the emphasis on entertainment mean that broadcast stations require relatively small investment in tangible assets and personnel. Bagdikian points out in *The Information Machines* that the average radio station has $162,000 invested in assets and a staff of 11, and the average television station has an investment of $1.93 million and 65 employees.[3]

By contrast, Bagdikian notes, the average newspaper has $4 million in assets, such as printing presses, and employs 200 persons. With newspapers, the mechanical production and distribution of the product require the major part of the budget and energies, whereas with broadcast stations these processes require a minor part.

While networking has economic advantages for broadcast stations, it limits the diversity of programming and information available to the public. To reach and hold national audiences of millions, centrally controlled programming must be based on interests that appeal to people of diverse ages and backgrounds in a variety of geographic areas. This common-denominator factor is important in broadcast priorities, particularly as they apply to news and public affairs.

News Programs. Broadcast news is unparalleled journalistically when it serves as a witness to actuality, reporting events "live" from the scene. It is most visible, and has its greatest impact, in coverage of drama such as an assassination, a fire, man's first step on the moon, and the historic meetings of Israeli and Egyptian leaders in 1977. The networks and stations "go all out" for such coverage.

Yet, news occupies an ambiguous position in broadcasting's commercial scheme: on the one hand, a first-class news operation is considered a mark of prestige; on the other, newscasts and public affairs documentary programs are allotted relatively little air time in comparison with entertainment. Very few newscasts are scheduled in the prime TV period, 8 to 11P.M.

The reason is plain. The overriding imperative in broadcasting is large audiences for advertising; and news, unless unusually different and dramatic, does not sustain audience interest for long periods. So newscasts are kept short and infrequent, normally (with the exception of all-news radio) scheduled at specific times scattered throughout the day.

The average television station reports 15 to 30 minutes (minus time for commercials) of news in the morning as people prepare for the day, again at noon, at 6 or 7 P.M., and at 10 or 11 P.M. Many larger TV stations in metropolitan areas run a half-hour of local news back-to-back with a half-hour network program that focuses on national and international news. In radio, the prevalent pattern on most stations is five minutes of news "every hour on the hour" between music and talk shows, with major emphasis on local news.

Generally considered the principal newscasts are the "7 O'Clock News" presented by the three TV networks. They feature the best-known, high-salaried anchorpersons and attract the largest national audiences. As a network "centerpiece," the evening news can help influence viewers in their station preference for other news programming, such as special reports, documentaries, panel shows, and even the morning news.

Given their short air time, average newscasts generally consist of a series of brief reports about 15 to 20 events. Few details are included about any individual event, and even the biggest news developments rarely rate more than a few minutes. In recent years, the networks and larger stations have included "mini-documentaries" on trends and unusual situations, along with lifestyle features.

One reason for the brevity is that it helps sustain an advantage that broadcast news offers: speed of delivery. Another is that only one news item can be presented at a time, and listeners uninterested in a particular item may tune out if too much time is spent on details. For the same reason, action and drama are stressed in an attempt to grab and hold audience interest.

The generally low priority given to broadcast news is reflected in the sparse manpower devoted to newsgathering, a costly process. In the industry as a whole there is relatively little original reportage, at least in comparison with newspapers and the press associations. The networks maintain correspondents in a few key American and foreign cities, and the larger stations have some roving local reporters; but the average station does not have sufficient staff to initiate much newsgathering. Broadcasting is not strong in crusading or investigative reporting.

Television news is severely handicapped by the limited availability of expensive camera crews, and logistical difficulties in getting bulky equipment set up at the scene of an event. For these reasons, much network news, for example, originates in urban centers where camera crews are located (New York, Washington, Chicago) and deals with events for which the crews can prepare in advance (news conferences, hearings, departures and arrivals).

For most stations the primary news sources are the newspapers and wire-service teleprinters (which are fed by newspapers). As a result, broadcast news is more of an echo than an independent voice in the average community. This is not to say that the overall news judgments are dissimilar. Uniform judgment of what is news, born of a common professional experience of journalists, means that newscasts on any given day compare closely in content with the front pages of the major daily newspapers. And, of course, radio and television add audio and visual dimensions that newspapers cannot duplicate. Achieving these dimensions claims much of the money and energy expended by broadcast news departments.

Because most stations air newscasts at the same hours, and because the newscasts hit only the high spots, broadcasting does not offer much choice in either listening times or content. Anyone who wants broadcast news must be near a radio or TV set at the commonly designated hours. National and international news comes from a central source, either a network or a press association teleprinter, and is therefore duplicative on all stations (the situation is similar with newspapers, except for large papers that have their own correspondents reporting from the scene). Broadcast local news follows the pattern of printed local news (often it is taken directly from the newspaper) and therefore tends to be similar on all stations within a community. Given these conditions, the size and nature of a station's audience for news, as likely as not, are determined by the personality and professionalism of the anchorperson who presents the news on the air.

The exception to the usual broadcast format is the all-news radio station, which offers news and information in continuous cycles around the clock. These stations require larger staffs than do the music-talk show stations, and therefore cost more to operate. In the mid-1970s there were close to 100 all-news radio stations, almost all in major metropolitan markets.

The staple of the all-news station is compact summaries of the day's news (WINS in New York had the slogan, "You give us twenty-two minutes and we'll give you the world"). The summaries are repeated periodically, with new developments continually replacing the older items. There is heavy emphasis on sports results, up-to-the-minute weather information, and traffic reports. Interspersed are occasional news commentaries and "soft" features on such subjects as homemaking, consumerism, and medicine.

Despite their limitations, commercial radio and television play a powerful role in the dissemination of news. They attract people who do not ordinarily spend much time with newspapers.

Public Broadcasting. Public, or noncommercial, television and radio are nonprofit. Unlike commercial broadcasting, they have no advertising; financing comes primarily from public sources, although some comes from private grants. Consequently, public broadcasting does not have the continual struggle for mass audiences and program ratings that commercial broadcasting has.

Programming aims at content not usually readily available in commercial broadcasting: "quality" cultural material, minority interests, educational instruction, and special public affairs such as congressional hearings and conferences. Public television represents about 15 percent of all TV program transmission in the United States; public radio accounts for an even smaller percentage of total radio transmission.

Public television in 1977 had 271 interconnected stations, but covered only 50 percent of the country because so many of the stations were on the hard-to-receive UHF frequency bands. Essentially there were four types of stations:

1. *Community stations*, licensed to nonprofit organizations, mostly in large cities. During the day they typically provide services for local school systems and children's programming; in the evening they offer a varied program of general interest for the community.

2. *School system stations*, whose primary function is to provide instructional programs as needed by the schools, with "public television" being something of a bonus.

3. *State and municipal stations*, which are responsive to the needs of the government units that established them.

4. *University stations*, whose chief responsibility is usually to the extension services of their institutions, although these stations also carry some local public affairs and national programming.

National public radio in 1977 had about 200 interconnected stations, the majority of them FM, which transmitted to 60 percent of the country. The system had its origins in educational radio, a network of university stations. Many stations are still owned by universities, but the overall ownership and programming patterns in the national system are similar to those in public television. In addition, there are more than 500 small noncommercial radio stations that are not considered part of the national interconnected system because they do not meet the minimum criteria for operations and programming.

The public broadcasting system is governed by national organizations: the Corporation for Public Broadcasting, a statutory body created by the 1967 Public Broadcasting Act, distributes federal funds to the system. The Public Broadcasting Service, a cooperative association of local stations, acts as a sort of network for distributing television programs. The National Public Radio Corporation produces, acquires, and distributes programs for its members.

The major reason that public broadcasting has not expanded its transmission and programming capabilities has been a chronic shortage of money. Unlike public broadcasting in other countries, the American system has not received strong financial support from the federal government. One argument against such support is that it could lead to government involvement in management and programming.

Actually, most of the money for public broadcasting has come from state and local tax sources, and from university budgets in the case of university-owned stations. Only the community stations have been able to generate any significant private support —from business and industry (which underwrite programs), foundations, individual subscribers, and television auctions. In general, the support has not been adequate for public broadcasting to fulfill its potential.

Cable Television. Since it was started in 1949–50, cable television has been heralded as the communications system of the future, comparable in importance to development of the railroad, the telephone, and over-the-air broadcasting. In addition to the services provided by aerial television, cable TV has the potential to give every home two-way communications leading to a variety of new services such as computer links and data-bank transmissions, facsimile reproduction of documents, education direct from the classroom, medical and social services, and crime protection systems.

Because of the obvious implications, development of such a system has raised complicated questions about control, regulation, and benefits. As a result, cable TV has been stymied by administrative and legislative uncertainties, opposition from commercial broadcasting interests, and high costs.

Technically, cable is not a broadcast service. Unlike regular television, which transmits signals through the air, cable television transmits via wires directly to the home. Cable TV systems pick up programs of broadcast stations by a central receiving antenna or by microwave radio relay, and deliver the programs to subscriber homes with a multichannel cable. Since 1965, cable systems have been regulated by the Federal Communications Commission, but they are not licensed as broadcast stations are. Operating franchises are granted by municipal governments.

Free of the air interferences of broadcast television, cable TV produces a clearer picture, is more reliable in reception, and has the capacity for many more channels. In the mid-1970s, some cable operators were offering as many as 30 channels, with up to 80 considered technically feasible in the future. Cable TV thus overcomes the basic limitation of broadcast television— channel scarcity.

Cable TV, or CATV (community antenna television), started in rural areas out of reach of regular TV, or where the terrain interferred with signals transmitted through the air. The system at first had one to three channels available, connected to sets at a nominal monthly fee. Before long, cable installations offered many channels and moved from remote areas into the cities and suburbs. Perhaps more important, programs could be imported from outside the normal over-the-air viewing area—a cheap and easy way to attract big audiences in major markets.

Initially unregulated by the government, ostensibly on the ground that it was not broadcasting, cable TV nevertheless presented new competition to the commercial broadcasting industry. With its programs imported from distant points, cable TV could "fractionalize" audiences normally tuned into commercial television and thus affect advertising income. Broadcasters argued that cable TV operators were violating copyright laws because they were not paying for the imported material. In addition, cable TV's capacity for local communication—delivering specific messages to specific audiences—could disrupt the existing commercial system of programming and advertising on a national or regional level.

Under pressure from the broadcasting industry and Congress, the FCC in 1965 assumed authority to regulate cable systems. Its first move was to rule that cable TV could not import distant signals into the top 100 markets. There then followed intense debate over policy questions related to public impact, industry structure, access, copyright, and impact on existing media and regulatory framework. In 1972, compromise agreements were reached among interested parties, and the way was opened for cable TV to develop in parallel with broadcasting. Broadcasting TV stations are no longer allowed to acquire cable TV franchises in the same city, and networks are prohibited from owning cable systems.

After its slow start, cable TV began to expand rapidly, with increased acceptance by local municipal authorities who award franchises. One reason was the ability of cable TV to provide channels for use by local governments and school systems and community organizations. Another was consumer desire for pay-television services from companies that present sports, movies, and special entertainment programs for an extra monthly charge.

In 1957, about 400,000 American homes had cable TV; in 1967 the number was 3 million. By 1977 there were more than 3,000 cable systems in the country, providing service to 12 million subscribers—about 17 percent of all television households. Industry experts estimated that the total would reach 20 million by 1980, and continue leaping upward after that, through use of domestic communications satellites for distribution. It seemed only a matter of time for cable to start fulfilling its potential for "wiring" the nation into new kinds of informational services.

MAGAZINES

Magazines essentially are a compromise between newspapers and books. Like newspapers, they inform, influence, entertain, and deliver advertising messages. Like books, they stress in-depth treatment of issues and situations, and generally are directed at specific audiences.

At least 8,000 American magazines are published for the

general public, the list continually vacillating because of additions and dropouts. They have an average total circulation of approximately 250 million per issue, and a total overlap readership of perhaps three times that number. Magazines fall into four broad categories: mass, news, class, and specialty. Together they cover virtually every kind of subject for every kind of audience.

Most magazines are businesses intended to yield profits. Closely bound to the marketing system, they derive their income from circulation sales and advertising. Many magazines are components of corporate enterprises or industrial conglomerates. About 70,000 people are employed in magazine publishing.

GROWTH OF TOTAL MAGAZINE CIRCULATION

1920	44 million
1940	95 million
1950	147 million
1960	190 million
1970	240 million

Role of Magazines. From their beginning in colonial times, magazines have supplemented newspapers as sources of information about American life. Broadly speaking, magazines expand on news, commentary, and entertainment features presented by newspapers. They are more concerned with trends than with day-to-day developments. Published weekly or monthly, magazines have the time and space to step back from immediate events, to put them in focus and to interpret their meaning. Often this involves a long investigation of an issue or a situation.

While newspapers are local and include a little of something for everybody, magazines, with few exceptions, are national in outlook and are more selective in the material they include. The typical magazine includes ten to twelve articles (some also include fiction), and each article generally is longer than the average newspaper story. Although some of the largest magazines have general appeal, most are directed at particular special-interest groups. There are magazines for homemakers, for business people, for scholars, for sports fans, for people who want their news digested, for people who want to be entertained, with fiction or otherwise.

Magazines are akin to books in that they are important tools in social research. Because of their in-depth reportage and diversity of information, magazines provide a historical catalog of American life. Because of their semipermanent physical nature, they are easily filed in libraries for reference.

Magazines evolved into a mass media because they are an adjunct to the country's marketing system. Having for the most part nationwide distribution, they are a major outlet for national advertising. The advertising generally parallels the editorial content. The typical magazine is written and edited to appeal to a homogeneous audience interested in a particular field or subject, and advertising is solicited from companies that want to reach that audience. Thus, a magazine designed for home-makers carries advertising mostly about products used in the home; a magazine about boating emphasizes nautical equipment.

Appeal of Magazines. As a mass medium, magazines do not have quite the blanket appeal of newspapers, radio, and tele-vision. The industry estimates that 85 percent of American adults read at least one magazine regularly. Some people read a half-dozen, but others rarely read any. Magazine reading essen-tially is a leisure-time activity, pursued for entertainment or supplementary information. It represents an expense that does not rate high in the family budget. Consequently, the purchasers of magazines as a whole tend to be the better-educated with comfortable incomes.

Types of Magazines. Although the best-known magazines are those of general interest sold on newsstands, the most numerous are specialized business and professional journals. Circulations for individual magazines range from the hundreds up to the millions. Some magazines have been published for a century or more; others enter and leave the market abruptly, depending on the times. A few publishers account for a high percentage of total magazine circulation and advertising, but they are not necessarily the most profitable.

It is difficult to classify some magazines, and there is much overlapping, but the principal categories are as follows:

Mass. As the classification implies, these magazines have large nationwide circulations of a million or more. They try to spread their reader appeal across different levels of education, background, income, and age. Some are of general interest, covering a variety of fields; others are more narrowly focused for special-interest audiences. All are written in a popular style.

The general consumer magazines once were the heart of the industry, but many have disappeared because of television's competition for national advertising, increased production and distribution costs, and fragmentation of the mass audience into special-interest groups. Among the notable victims were *Collier's*, the old *Saturday Evening Post, Life,* and *Look.* The most prominent survivor is the *Reader's Digest,* which sold 18.5 million copies a month in the United States in the mid-1970s. *Parade* and *Family Weekly,* which are distributed with some large-city Sunday newspapers, and Sunday magazines of such individual papers as the *New York Times,* fit into this category.

Many magazines designed for particular purposes or readership have cultivated mass audiences. They include *TV Guide,* which has a weekly circulation of 18 million; women's magazines, such as *Cosmopolitan, Ladies' Home Journal, McCall's,* and *Good Housekeeping;* men's, such as *Playboy;* family living, such as *Better Homes and Gardens;* farm, such as *Farm Journal* and *Successful Farming;* how-to-do-it, such as *Popular Mechanics* and *Popular Science;* personalities, such as *People* and *Us;* history and culture, such as *National Geographic* and *Smithsonian.* Some of these magazines in recent years have expanded their editorial content to include subjects of general interest and thus have attracted a broad cross-section of readers.

News. These weekly publications, which are mass magazines in terms of circulation, combine the characteristics of newspapers and magazines that offer longer articles. They summarize the week's news, add background and interpretation, and present it all in a neat, liberally illustrated, easy-to-read package. In addition, in their "back-of-the-book" sections, they discuss trends in such fields as education, religion, social behavior, law, sports, and performing arts.

The newsmagazines aim at mass appeal, but their readers generally have a strong interest in contemporary affairs that sets them apart from the average American. The bulk of the audience is comprised of college-educated, upper-income opinion setters who, in their busy lives, want to catch up on the news and trends in a hurry. In the mid-1970s, *Time,* the oldest newsmagazine, had a circulation of 4.25 million; *Newsweek*, with an almost identical format, had 2.9 million. *U.S. News & World Report*, which is not tied to developing news events as much as the other two, had a circulation of under 2 million.

As the newspapers and wire services have added background and interpretation of their own in recent years, *Time* and *Newsweek* have broken away from the set formula of repackaged news. They have striven for "freshness" through original reporting, and have given new attention to long news features in the form of "cover stories."

CLASS. Sometimes called quality magazines, these publications are written for select audiences. The typical reader is well educated and interested in literature and public affairs. Though they have smaller circulations than the mass magazines, the class magazines tend to have more significant influence because so many of their readers are opinion leaders. Content usually is a mixture of factual accounts, scholarly essays, opinion, reviews, fiction, and sometimes poetry.

Among the most widely read in this category are the *New Yorker, Saturday Review, Harper's,* and *Atlantic*. Smaller magazines of opinion include the *New Republic,* the *Nation,* and *National Review*.

SPECIALTY. In number of individual publications, these magazines represent the largest segment of the magazine industry. They are written for readers interested in a specific subject or field, and include detailed information and technical data usually not offered in the other types of magazines. Many are not widely known because they are not displayed on newsstands but have controlled mail circulation.

At least 2,500 publications are devoted to business, led by the well-known general business or business news magazines: *Business Week, Fortune, Nation's Business,* and *Forbes*. The rest are journals, published by business associations or commercial publishers, designed to help people in businesses and professions, from industrial manufacturing and stock brokerage to medicine and engineering.

Other specialty magazines and newsletters cover every interest and activity imaginable: religion and education, law and political affairs, communications and the performing arts, archaeology and anthropology, social behavior and science, hobbies and recreation, animals and travel.

Specialty publications play a journalistic role beyond their intended readership. They are an important source of tips and research material for stories that appear in the mass news media.

Editorial Operations. The bulk of magazine content is factual, or nonfiction; only a few consumer magazines carry fiction, now that television offers fictionalized entertainment. Most magazines function with small editorial staffs, mainly editors and a few staff writers. Much of their material is produced by free-lance writers and photographers who are paid on a fee basis. The notable exception to this arrangement is the newsmagazine, which is produced almost entirely by an in-house staff. *Time* and *Newsweek* have large newsgathering operations, exceeded in size perhaps only by the *New York Times*. Their editorial operations have been tabbed "journalism by committee," with the information gathered by one group of journalists, written by a second group, and edited by a third.

Circulation and Advertising. Almost every magazine costs more to produce and distribute than the price it yields from the consumer. There is a general price ceiling that is acceptable in the market. The difference usually is covered by advertising, which also produces the profits.

Magazines are distributed primarily by newsstands and by mail. Each method has disadvantages. Newsstand sales are not certain; often they are an impulse purchase, putting a premium on provocative and interesting covers. Mail subscriptions are subject to postal rates, which have been going up steadily. Distribution is an intricate and costly process because copies of each issue must be delivered nationwide by a fixed date each week or month.

Circulation is vital to attracting advertising for consumer magazines. A publisher must assure an advertiser either a mass audience with general interests or a smaller but established audience likely to be interested in the product the advertiser wants to sell. Advertising rates are based largely on the size of circulation, rising as circulation increases. Many advertisers cannot afford the rates of mass magazines, so they turn to the smaller, special-audience publications.

A huge circulation does not necessarily mean profitability, because of the law of diminishing returns. The income received from added subscribers may not offset the cost of supplying those subscribers. *Life* and *Look* had circulations of over 7 million but succumbed in the early 1970s to overburdening production and distribution costs and changing public tastes that altered the patterns of advertising.

Most of the smaller, scholarly publications do not rely on advertising. They are subsidized by professional societies, universities, or other nonprofit groups, or are paid for out of membership fees.

The cost of starting a magazine is small, in contrast to the heavy investment needed for newspaper publishing or broadcasting. In addition to having minimal staffs and modest offices, magazines ordinarily do not invest in expensive printing presses but let out their printing on contract. Thus, new magazines can enter the market relatively easily, and publications with small circulations can compete.

A few large publishers dominate the field in terms of circulation and money spent. Time, Inc. publishes *Time, Fortune, Sports Illustrated, Money*, and *People*. Hearst publishes such moneymakers as *Cosmopolitan, Good Housekeeping*, and *Popular Mechanics*. Meredith Publishing Company has *Better Homes and Gardens* and *Successful Farming*. McGraw-Hill puts out *Business Week* and about 50 other business and trade publications.

Some of the large publishers are diversified beyond magazines. Time, Inc. publishes books in a dozen languages, produces educational materials, owns television stations and paper companies, and has movie investments. McGraw-Hill sells films, instructional systems, books, investment services, and computerized information services. Reader's Digest Association turns out textbooks and almanacs, special how-to books, and phonograph records.

PUBLIC RELATIONS AND ADVERTISING

The purpose of public relations and advertising is to sell something, whether it be an image, an idea, or a product. Although neither activity is the work of the journalist, each is integrally involved in the journalistic process. Public relations personnel provide much of the information about government, institutional, and corporate life. Advertisers provide the bulk of the economic base of the media. Since World War II the two fields have grown extensively.

Public Relations. There are many definitions of public relations. One that has been widely accepted came from Cyril W. Plattes, manager of the department of public services for General Mills, who said that public relations is that responsibility and function of management which (1) analyzes public interest and determines public attitudes; (2) identifies and interprets policies and programs of an organization; and (3) executes a program of action to merit acceptance and good will.

To carry out that function, virtually every corporation, company, government agency, public institution, politician, university, church, athletic team, trade union, community group, movie star, fund-raising organization, and communications medium has a staff of "contact people" and/or writers and editors to disseminate information about its employer and to promote the employer's cause. The staff pursues its objective through personal contact, written press releases, organizational magazines, films, staged events such as press conferences and panel discussions, and any other means it thinks will be effective.

Much of the public-relations attention is directed at the news media, which serve as a channel to the public. Newspapers, broadcasting stations, and magazines receive a steady flow of press releases. (In their sociological study of the journalist and his work, *The News People*, John W. C. Johnstone, Edward J. Slawski, and William W. Bowman estimate that 1.3 million news releases are sent each week to the media throughout the country.)[4] Reporters are invited to press conferences and other events arranged by public relations personnel. The purpose is to gain mention in a paper or on the air of the cause the public relations personnel represent.

PR activity can be useful to the journalist. It can provide information and viewpoints necessary to a news story, and thus save time and energy. It can provide tips to the news. It can obtain access to important news sources. This is particularly true with government agencies and large corporations. The problem for the journalist is to make sure that the news has not been distorted, manipulated, or fabricated.

Although the public-relations, or publicity, function has existed since the early part of the twentieth century, it has expanded greatly with the growth of industry, government, communications, and general complexity of life since mid-century. The competition for attention and sales, whether it be related to soap or politician, opened the way for imagemakers. In the mid-1970s more than 110,000 people were employed in the field.

The largest area of public-relations work is in corporate business. Most business and industrial firms have their own public-relations staffs, as do government agencies and institutional organizations. In addition, there are independent public-relations firms and counselors who provide PR service on contract. A large percentage of public-relations personnel formerly worked for the news media.

Advertising. Advertising is important to the communications field in two ways: First, with its distinct approach and format, it provides the public with marketing information necessary to keep the American consumer economy going. Second, it is by far the largest source of financial support for the mass media.

There are many definitions of the role of advertising in the marketing of products, but one of the most-quoted is the following by Frederick R. Gamble, former president of the American Association of Advertising Agencies.

Advertising is the counterpart in distribution of the machine in production. By the use of machines, our production of goods and services multiples the selling effort. Advertising is the great accelerating force in distribution. Reaching many people rapidly at low cost, advertising speeds up sales, turns prospects into customers in large numbers and at high speed. Hence, in a mass-production and high-consumption economy, advertising has the greatest opportunity and the great responsibility for finding customers.[5]

Advertisements for use in newspapers, magazines, and broadcasting are not prepared by staffs of the media; even when a medium wants to advertise itself, it usually goes to an outside specialist. The media do, however, have space or time salespeople, and most have national sales representatives to obtain advertising for them.

Advertisements are planned, created, and disseminated by special personnel of firms or institutions in conjunction with advertising agencies working under contract. The process involves intensive analysis and research of both product and market. Advertising breaks down into two broad categories: consumer, which is designed to sell a product or service directly; and institutional, which is aimed more at promoting "good will."

Since World War II, advertising in the United States has grown rapidly in tandem with the growth of the consumer economy. Research and development in industry, government, and education have led to more efficient manufacturing and countless new products in such fields as plastics and electronics. By the mid-1970s, American business was spending more than $25 billion annually to sell its products. To deal with the large volume of advertising, there were about 400,000 people employed in the field: 75,000 in 4,800 advertising agencies, 100,000 in the mass media, and the rest in manufacturing, service, retail, and wholesale firms of all types and sizes.

NOTES

1. Ben H. Bagdikian, *The Information Machines* (New York: Harper Colophon Books, 1971), p. 69.
2. *Ibid.*, pp. 72–74.
3. *Ibid.*, p. 170.
4. John W. C. Johnstone, Edward J. Slawski, and William W. Bowman, *The News People* (Urbana: University of Illinois Press, 1976), p. 19.
5. Quoted in Edwin Emery, et al., *Introduction to Mass Communications* (New York: Dodd, Mead & Company, Inc., 1973), p. 308.

SUGGESTED READING

Bagdikian, Ben H. *The Information Machines*. New York: Harper Colophon Books, 1971.

Brown, Les. *Television: The Business Behind the Box*. New York: Harcourt Brace Jovanovich, Inc., 1971.

Emery, Edwin, Ault, Phillip H., and Agee, Warren K. *Introduction to Mass Communications*. New York: Dodd, Mead & Company, 1973.

Friendly, Fred. W. *Due to Circumstances Beyond Our Control*. New York: Random House, 1967.

Peterson, Theodore. *Magazines in the Twentieth Century*. Urbana: University of Illinois Press, 1964.

5

People in the News Media

As the novelist was the conscience and spokesman for humanity in the nineteenth century, so is the journalist in the twentieth century. The journalist no longer is simply a chronicler of events, a recorder of "history in the making"; he is in addition an analyst and interpreter of the events he reports. He may be a reporter on the street, but he also may be a Washington or foreign correspondent, an editorial writer, a columnist, a specialist on a complex subject, or an editor who rarely leaves the newsroom.

The average modern journalist is a young, white, middle-class male who is motivated more by the nature of his job than the money he receives to perform it. He is better educated and better qualified than his predecessor, and more than likely attended a journalism school. Landing his first job was not easy because journalism in the 1970s was a popular field.

CAREER OF JOURNALIST

When he retired in 1977 after 33 years with the *New York Times*, including stints as a foreign correspondent, managing editor, and chief of the Washington bureau, Clifton Daniel said,

"There's no profession that offers you more variety in life or more excitement."[1]

Wide Appeal. Not many journalists' careers can match Daniel's in variety and excitement, but a career in news has always had wide appeal. This is partially due to the image, fostered by movies and novels, of romance, glamour, mystery—of the reporter dashing off to exotic places, rubbing elbows with important people, and uncovering the answer to the problem. Actually, much of the work in journalism has always been routine and tedious, and what romance and glamour there have been were lessened by the coming of automation to the newsroom and institutionalization of the news process. Still, perhaps as much as any other field, modern journalism offers the stimulation of action, the challenge of discovery, the sense of creativity.

Ben Bagdikian once told a group of journalism students that there are two great characteristics that make news work worthwhile: First, journalists are forced to keep learning, to enter new worlds, to see life from yet another perspective. Second, they are supposed to say what things are *really* like.

"What you do every day is not fill out forms, or project a pleasing personality, or tighten a lug on an assembly line or sell another computer part," he said. "What you do every day is use your intellect and your talents to create something that is new and unique to you."[2]

Prestige and Power. Out of all this emerges a sense of participation, of prestige, of power that comes from acting as the public's surrogate. How much prestige and power a journalist has depends on his or her particular position, of course. Few journalists have great power as individuals; but virtually all journalists have some power as parts of the collective process of gathering, preparing, and presenting the news in print or broadcasting. As communications authority William L. Rivers has put it, "Every journalist affects lives."

As chonicler, the journalist keeps people informed about what is happening in their community and the rest of the world so that they can plan their lives.

As critic, the journalist serves as the public's watchdog, monitoring the thinking and activities of influential decisionmakers. He investigates and, whenever possible, reveals the wrongs in society—and also points out the rights.

As innovator, the journalist explores alternative ways of doing things and suggests reforms when he thinks they are needed.

As leader, the journalist helps shape opinions—and thus society—by the selection of the news he reports, by his interpretation of events, by his monitoring and initiative toward reform.

Increasing Responsibility. While the journalist has always to some degree been chronicler, critic, innovator, and leader, his role has become increasingly significant, and his responsibility increasingly greater, as government and society have become more complex, particularly since World War II. Nowadays there is a continuous flow of new developments and ideas to report and interpret: in science, urban affairs, industry, politics, international affairs. People are bombarded by information from every side, and they look to the journalist to sort things out and explain them. As James Reston of the *New York Times* has said, "Today's reporter is forced to become an educator more concerned with explaining the news than with being the first on the scene."[3]

Journalism educator John Hohenberg asserts in *The Professional Journalist* that the impact of the journalist on public opinion is one of the strongest motivating forces in American society: "What he thinks, what he says, and what he does now can exert an enormous influence on a mass audience, including those far beyond the borders of his own land."[4]

NATURE OF THE JOURNALIST AND HIS JOB

In the mid-1970s approximately 70,000 full-time salaried journalists were employed by news organizations. About 75 percent of them worked for newspapers and magazines, 20 percent for television and radio, and 5 percent for the press associations (or wire services), according to *The News People*, a comprehensive sociological study of journalists by John W. C. Johnstone, Edward J. Slawski, and William W. Bowman.[5] In addition, there were at least an equal number of people who contributed to the overall news process as part-time correspondents, free-lance writers, or public-relations persons.

Changing Image. The traditional image of the journalist is the reporter, pad and pencil in hand, taking notes frenetically at the scene of a fire or highway accident. The reporter, to be sure, is the backbone of journalism, whether he be covering the police beat, city hall, the White House, or a foreign capital; but the functions of a journalist in modern times have gone far beyond the traditional image.

With television and radio now so prominent in the news system, the journalist may be holding a tape recorder or microphone or minicamera rather than a pad and pencil. With the complexity of modern life, he may be a science specialist assigned to a conference on computers, rather than a fire. With interpretation of the news so essential, he may be an editorial writer or columnist who analyzes, rather than reports, the news. He may be an executive editor or a copy editor who rarely leaves the newsroom; in fact, the majority of newspeople are not involved firsthand in reporting the world's events and evolution but instead spend most of their time processing information structured by others.

Job Categories. A journalist has a choice of three basic roles to play in the news business. He or she can be a reporter; an editor who edits and otherwise processes the news gathered by the reporter; or a supervisory editor who manages the overall editorial operation. Reporting is regarded as an "outside" function because the reporter spends much of his time out in the community; the other two functions are regarded as "inside" jobs because the work is done within the organization. This manpower pattern evolved with newspapers, but it also applies loosely to broadcast news operations.

The most common single category of activity is reporting. According to *The News People*, reporters are almost evenly divided between those who cover beats (such as police, politics, labor) and those who cover a variety of topics (general-assignment reporters). Beats are more prevalent with newspapers than with radio and television. Because they spend most of their time mingling with people outside the office, and have their names on their stories, reporters generally have more recognition than the "inside" journalists. Editorial writers, columnists, and commentators, as "initiators" of news and information, are also classified in this category.

The more anonymous function is performed by the "inside" people who process the work initiated by reporters and other writers. These journalists, primarily copy editors, stand between the reporters and the critical public. They check the factual accuracy and content clarity of stories, add information from research if needed, polish the writing and rewrite portions of stories if necessary, edit stories for proper length, and write headlines. Because of the sensitive function they perform, copy editors sometimes are referred to as the heart of the news operation.

The third function is editorial management. This is the responsibility of the top editors, such as the executive editor, managing editor, and city editor. These executives establish and execute the overall policies and editorial direction of the news operation, decide which news events should be covered and reported to the public, and supervise the editorial personnel in achieving the finished product.

There is considerable overlap among the three functions, the extent depending on the size of newspaper or broadcast station. In a small operation, the editorial boss is likely to report, write, and process regularly as well as manage; in a large operation, such as the *New York Times* or CBS News, the top editors rarely write or process because they are busy planning and coordinating.

Journalism is similar to other fields in that experience and longevity are key determining factors in the assignment of tasks. Reporting is the usual entry to journalism, and the processing and managing tasks generally come later. Perhaps four-fifths of all journalists start as reporters; if they stay in the news business, a large percentage of them are likely to move into "inside" decisionmaking jobs as they grow older and gain experience. In general, then, reporters are younger than the "inside" personnel.

Journalistic Profile. The broad characteristics of journalists were found by *The News People* to be the following:

AGE. Journalists tend to be young on the average, although relatively few are under twenty-five. The late entry into the field is probably explained by the higher-than-average level of educational preparation for journalism. A majority of journalists, 56.3 percent, are in their twenties or thirties, and broadcast newspersons are younger (median age 30.8 years) than their print counterparts (38.1 years).

SEX. Although women have been entering journalism in increasing numbers, they were still outnumbered four to one by men in the 1970s (compared to a two-to-one ratio in the total full-time labor force). Female representation was higher in print journalism than in broadcast, ranging from a high of 30.4 percent in newsmagazines to a low of 4.8 percent in radio. Female representation seems likely to increase because female enrollment in journalism schools is high; the starting enrollment of 155 students in the 1977–78 class at Columbia University's Graduate School of Journalism included 85 women.

Despite some movement toward equality of task and responsibility, perhaps a quarter of female journalists are dealing with news traditionally described as of interest to women: fashion and lifestyle topics. Relatively few are in managerial posts with power to make policy and hire and fire. One reason cited for this situation is that, since women as a group are latecomers to journalism, few have acquired the experience and longevity deemed necessary for supervisory positions. Critics claim that the basic reason is lingering male discrimination against female journalists.

The News People study seems to support the critics' view. The report stated:

> Evidence both from this and other studies makes it clear that career opportunities for men and women in the news media differ markedly: Men have better chances of being recruited into the media to begin with; they are more likely to be assigned "important" news beats early in their careers; and they have much better chances of eventual promotion into positions of organizational responsibility.[6]

SOCIAL ORIGINS. Journalists tend to come from the established and dominant cultural groups in American society. They are overwhelmingly white, and three-fourths have had middle- or upper-middle-class backgrounds in urban surroundings. Only about 4 percent of journalists are black (compared with 12 percent in the population at large), and a third of these work in the black press.

EDUCATION. Although there are no formal educational requirements for entering journalism, since World War II news organizations have leaned more and more toward college graduates in their recruitment. In the 1970s, 58 percent of journalists had college diplomas and 8 percent held advanced degrees. Older journalists, long in the field, had less college education on the average than their younger colleagues. Journalists with special education in fields such as science, law, and economics were in demand as the news became more complex. It was not uncommon, for example, for a large news organization to have a doctor reporting medical news or a lawyer writing about legal affairs.

Geographic Distribution. The heaviest concentrations of news manpower are in the northeastern megalopolises, principally the metropolitan New York area, and to a lesser degree on the West Coast. This pattern reflects the fact that the news industry started in the Northeast, which was the center of population and commerce, and the major share of production and distribution facilities developed in that region. The broadcast networks, newsmagazines, and wire services, as well as some of the leading newspapers, are headquartered in New York. News manpower also is concentrated in urban areas, with the highest per-capita representation in cities of less than a million people.

The impact of the relationship between the characteristics of journalists and the nature of mass news in American society is suggested by this statement in *The News People*:

> News is ultimately what newsmen make it, and what finds its way into the news system is by necessity a reflection of where news is gathered and what those who gather it define as newsworthy. It is perhaps more than accidental, then, that affairs and events emanating from urban places tend to dominate American news; that news in large measure reflects men's rather than women's definitions of newsworthiness; and that the affairs of established groups in the society are virtually always defined as more newsworthy than those of minorities and disadvantaged groups.[7]

Working Conditions. In the old days of journalism, newspapermen were pictured as an independent and footloose bunch who went anywhere, any time, for a scoop. The stereotype of the *Front Page* pattern was the reporter, hat brim up and cigarette dangling, shouting "copy!" as he grabbed a glass of whiskey from his desk. However true the stereotype, yesterday's journalists, employed by smaller organizations than today's corporate enterprises, pursued "personal" journalism through unstructured lives, long and irregular duty hours, and low pay.

Today it's quite different, although conditions vary considerably according to the size and location of the news organization. Scoops are still important, but not as urgent as they used to be.

The average journalist doesn't roam very far from home, and might be mistaken for a lawyer or accountant on his way to the office. Unless he works for a small organization, he is not really an individual communicator, but a synchronized part of a collective newsgathering machine. About two-thirds of today's journalists work for organizations that are incorporated into larger chains, groups, or networks. While many still work long and unusual hours, most have set schedules that include specified days off and normal vacations. Their offices are modern and comfortable. Their wages are on a par with those of most other white-collar occupations, even though only a minority of the nation's newsroom personnel are represented by unions.

"Once an ill-paid and rather raffish trade for disillusioned idealists, journalism is now respectable and reasonably remunerative," said Jeremy Main in an article about journalism, "A Career That's Hit Its Heyday," which appeared in *Money* magazine.[8]

The routine and tedious aspects of their jobs aside, most journalists find their work interesting and rewarding on the whole. They face new situations every day. They have opportunities to meet important and interesting people, and to grapple with vital social and political issues. They derive gratification from performing a public service, however small their contribution. While they work constantly under deadline pressures, they consider this to be part of "being in on the action."

Within this broad context, most journalists develop a feeling of camaraderie toward their colleagues, of belonging to the news fraternity. As one young editor of a small newspaper said in the *Money* magazine article, "Newspapers tend to build up a sense of community within themselves. They tend to be very enjoyable places to work."

Pay Scale. There are wide variations in journalists' pay, depending on organizational and geographic factors, the characteristics of the newspersons, and the functions they perform. The highest salaries are paid by the large metropolitan daily newspapers, the major newsmagazines, and the broadcast networks.

In 1975, according to data from the Newspaper Guild, annual salaries for beginning reporters on unionized newspapers ranged from a low of $6,000 to a high of $19,500. Scales at nonunionized papers were somewhat lower. A typical starting salary was around $8,000. After three to five years of experience, an average reporter or photographer could earn up to $17,000. At major publications such as *Time* magazine, the *New York Times*, the *Los Angeles Times*, and the *Washington Post*, some editorial salaries exceeded $40,000 a year. The same was true of the television networks and leading TV stations. The highest annual editorial salaries, as much as $300,000 to $400,000, were paid to television network anchorpeople.

Generally, salaries are somewhat higher in broadcast news than in print; the national weekly newsmagazines exceed all other sectors. Pay is better in television than in radio, and better on daily newspapers than on weeklies. Usually, the larger the community and news organization, the higher is the pay scale. Journalists who perform managerial duties and supervise employees command higher salaries than those who do not. On the average, men receive better pay than do women.

Geographically, salaries in journalism reflect regional differences found within the labor force as a whole. According to the findings in *The News People*, the highest pay levels are in the Pacific states, the lowest in the South. The Middle Atlantic states, which constitute the heart of the news industry, rank third.

Job Mobility. Studies have found that job satisfaction and career commitments are quite high throughout journalism. Some old-timers have been with the same news organizations for decades. Still, as a group, journalists, particularly the younger ones, are more mobile than workers in most other occupations. And the trend toward centralization, automation, and bureaucracy has introduced factors that seem to affect job satisfaction.

The Johnstone-Slawski-Bowman study found that more journalists prefer to work in small news organizations than in large ones.[9] The reason is that small organizations offer editorial personnel more individual freedom to select the stories they work on, and less interference from the copy processors. At the same time, however, journalists like to be identified with prestigious organizations that pay higher salaries and offer greater opportunity for advancement.

Therein lies the dilemma that generates mobility and dissatisfaction. The prosperous, prestigious news organizations tend to be the big ones that allow less personal autonomy because of the increasing centralization and collective activity. As the Johnstone-Slawski-Bowman study points out, many ambitious journalists switch jobs in their effort to get ahead, but in so doing they "must trade off certain of their professional ideals for higher earnings and better opportunities for professional recognition."

Job mobility is greater in broadcast journalism than in print, and there is relatively little crossing over between the two. Job shifts tend to be between organizations within broadcast or print, and the principal reasons for the shifts are higher pay and wider professional recognition.

Job Qualifications. Editors and other experts have cited a myriad of qualities that an aspiring journalist should have to seek a career in the field. Some say curiosity, a "nose for news." Others say integrity and courage, or vitality and vigilance, or diligence to pursue the truth whatever that may take. Still others say an ability to write with style and a disciplined mind to understand and relate the complex issues of modern times. In *The Professional Journalist,* John Hohenberg sums up what he considers the minimum requirements:

- A thorough education, sound training, and discipline.
- Familiarity with the basic skills of the journalist.
- The will to work at tasks that are sometimes frustrating and often unrewarding.
- A deep respect for one's personal and professional integrity.[10]

Job Preparation. Journalism does not have a set of requirements or procedures (in the manner of law and medicine, for example) to certify qualified newspeople. There are many ways to enter the field. Some journalists have gone to work right out of high school. Others have chosen to get professional training first, or a broad substantive background. Still others have taken jobs in other fields and then switched to journalism.

There is wide agreement, however, that the days of entering news work as an "apprentice" out of high school are largely gone. Today, with the expansion of higher education, most news organizations prefer college graduates and have a large reservoir of applicants.

There is no clear consensus on the best educational preparation. One view is that a liberal arts education is sufficient. Most editors and newsroom executives agree that a background in such subjects as political science, economics, government, history, sociology, and English is desirable. With such a background, many experts believe, an enterprising person can learn the news techniques "on the job." The trouble with this approach, Ben Bagdikian points out, is that "newspapers and broadcasters refuse to do systematic on-the-job journalistic training for inexperienced beginners because it would require money and the time of senior professionals."[11]

A second view is that liberal arts should be combined with journalism education. Most undergraduate journalism programs are set up with this combination, and graduate programs assume that students come to them already prepared in liberal arts. Proponents of journalism education argue that a graduate of a journalism school goes to his first job familiar with the rudiments of urban reporting, copy editing, communications law and ethics, and the new electronics technology being installed in many newsrooms. More important, the proponents say, these graduates will have an understanding of the proper role of journalism in society, and knowledge of the different approaches taken by the media to perform that role.

Journalism enrollments at colleges and universities have soared in recent years—going from 11,000 students in 1960 to 64,000 in 1976. Enrollments increased by 93 percent between 1970 and 1975. The conventional explanation for the popularity has been the uncovering of Watergate scandals by two young *Washington Post* reporters, Robert Woodward and Carl Bernstein. While the "Woodstein" success may have galvanized many young people into pursuing journalism, Professor Paul V. Peterson of Ohio State University, who compiles national figures on journalism majors, had another answer:

> The big boom began from 1971 to 1972 and it happened because young people had already seen journalism as a way to change the world. It was the beginning of consumer journalism. People who would have originally majored in English felt that even though they might have no intention of working for a newspaper, they might be able to help change the world if they mastered basic journalism skills.[12]

As with just about everything else in journalism, education for journalism varies widely. Nearly 600 two-year community colleges offer courses, but the instruction rarely is more than an introduction to the field. At least 200 colleges and universities have departments or schools of journalism or communications, some of which offer programs covering most phases of journalism and allied work. Of these, 65 are accredited by the American Council on Education for Journalism. A few that are usually listed among the leaders are (in alphabetical order) Columbia, Minnesota, Missouri, Northwestern, and Stanford.

Enrollments range from fewer than 100 to 3,000 majors at the University of Texas School of Communications. Most of the programs are at the undergraduate level, but several lead to graduate degrees. The main emphasis in the programs, in terms of courses offered, is news-editorial, followed by advertising, broadcasting, and public relations.

Although there is debate over the value of journalism education, the media in the 1970s leaned toward journalism schools and departments in their campus searches for new talent. According to studies, including those of the Newspaper Fund, a nonprofit foundation that encourages careers in journalism, roughly 70 percent of the recruits hired by the news media directly from college were journalism graduates.

Whatever the path taken by the aspiring journalist, professionals agree that he should get a head start by working for his high school or college newspaper or radio station. This preliminary exposure will tell the student whether he really wants to pursue journalism as a career. If he is convinced, then he has some basic training on which to build.

Increasingly, journalists are finding that their educational needs and desires do not end with obtaining a job. With the trend toward specialization, many working newspeople are continuing their education with courses in such subjects as writing, economics, law, and public affairs. Some colleges and journalism schools have special mid-career programs tailored for journalists who take a leave of absence from their jobs to study.

Job Opportunities. Although the job market for journalists in the 1970s has generally been described as tight, there are hundreds of openings across the country. The normal turnover and attrition are considerable. Moreover, the growing size of newspapers and the increase in the number of specialty and trade magazines have expanded the job market in print. Advertising and public relations have also been expanding at a steady rate. The situation in broadcasting has been more static, but openings do exist.

The trouble with all this is that the available jobs are not the kinds that most budding journalists want. They are not with prestigious organizations in the big time; they are with small organizations away from the East and West coasts where so many aspiring newspeople prefer to settle. In addition, the jump in journalism school enrollments has meant stiffer competition for the openings that do exist, and many graduates have to forgo news organizations, at least in their first jobs.

Here is the picture in brief:

NEWSPAPERS. Roughly 80 percent of newspaper beginners start as reporters. They don't move into editing and other processing jobs until they have some experience. Daily newspapers hire about 58 percent of the recruits to the news business, but the overwhelming majority are in small communities. Weeklies take an additional 14 percent. Because the journalism manpower pool is now extensive, virtually all metropolitan dailies demand four to five years of experience, or a useful specialty talent, as the minimum requisite to hiring. "Go out into the boondocks and get some experience," is the familiar admonition to beginners.

WIRE SERVICES. The wire services (Associated Press and United Press International) traditionally have been one of the best starting points and training grounds for journalists. In the past they have hired young people with little or no professional experience and have trained them to work with speed and conciseness in all phases of news work. The usual route for the recruit has been from a "line" bureau in a medium-sized city to a major bureau in a big city. Turnover has always been heavy, but staffs are small. Wire services employ only 5 percent of the total editorial personnel in the country. In the 1970s, like the newspapers, the wire services have had a surplus of job applicants and have required one to two years experience for hiring in many cases.

BROADCASTING. Television and radio employ 20 percent of the 70,000 journalists in the United States. Staffs are small. Of all broadcast journalists, 57 percent work for stations with ten or fewer full-time editorial employees; 36 percent of radio journalists are in news departments of one, two, or three persons. Openings for beginners are relatively rare in radio, and even rarer in television.

As with print, the best place to start is with a small station in a small community, where the journalist's responsibility consists mainly of preparing and presenting newscasts directly from the press association wire. The usual job course is to gain experience at a small station, progress to reporting at larger stations, and eventually move into production and managerial responsibilities at a large station or network. Because broadcasting requires knowledge of special equipment and newsroom techniques, employment chances are enhanced by broadcast training at a journalism school.

MAGAZINES. The major newsmagazines are one of the toughest markets to crack, and few beginners succeed. An occasional well-qualified journalism graduate may land a job as a researcher and eventually work up to reporter or writer status. Generally, though, the newsmagazines have the luxury of hiring experienced personnel from newspapers and the wire services.

General magazines offer opportunities for exceptionally talented writers and editors, but staffs are small. These magazines employ more women than any other print sector. The best way to get attention is to sell some free-lance articles as proof of talent. Trade magazines and company publications are an expanding field with openings, and they provide the best opportunity to learn the complex mechanical techniques of editing and design.

ADVERTISING AND PUBLIC RELATIONS. Although these fields are not strictly news activities, they utilize journalistic skills and offer opportunities for the beginner. Both fields are expanding steadily and thus have openings. An increasing number of journalism graduates are finding jobs in advertising and public relations.

NOTES

1. The *New York Times*, Oct. 5, 1977, p. A22.
2. "The Joy of Journalism," *Bulletin* of the American Society of Newspaper Editors, Nov./Dec. 1976, p. 9.
3. Fred W. Friendly, *Due to Circumstances Beyond Our Control* (New York: Random House, 1967), p. 199.
4. John Hohenberg, *The Professional Journalist* (New York: Holt, Rinehart and Winston, Inc., 1969), p. 4.
5. John W. C. Johnstone, Edward J. Slawski, and William W. Bowman, *The News People* (Urbana: University of Illinois Press, 1976), p. 19.
6. *Ibid.*, p. 137.
7. *Ibid.*, p. 28.
8. "A Career That's Hit Its Heyday," *Money*, April 1977, pp. 46–52.
9. Johnstone *et al.*, p. 184.
10. Hohenberg, pp. 5–6.
11. "Woodstein U.," *Atlantic Monthly*, March 1977, p. 92.
12. "The Week in Review," *New York Times*, March 6, 1977, p. 11.

SUGGESTED READING

Johnstone, John W. C., Slawski, Edward J., and Bowman, William W. *The News People*. Urbana: University of Illinois Press, 1976.

Shiller, Herbert I. *The Mind Managers*. Boston: Beacon, 1973.

Talese, Gay. *The Kingdom and the Power*. New York: The World Publishing Company, 1969.

6

Criticism of the Media

Attacking the press is an old American custom—even in the best of times for the press. In the 1970s, caught up in the information explosion and buoyed by its role in the Watergate affair, the press was vested with probably more power, prestige, and glamour than ever before. Paradoxically, it also was the target of widespread criticism. While Watergate publicized the press's strengths, it also focused attention on journalism's weaknesses. Polls suggested considerable public distrust of the media, and there were moves to curtail the press's First Amendment freedoms.

Some complaints were new, the by-products of the information explosion and the consolidation of the information machine: The media were too big and powerful, too tightly controlled by too few people, too standardized in their presentation of the news. Some complaints were familiarly old: The media paid too much attention to trivia, gossip, sex, and violence, and not enough to significant social, economic, and political trends.

The media, historically averse to self-examination and self-reform, began to take note of the criticism. Some newspapers and magazines opened their columns to ombudsmen and media

123

analysts, and the nongovernmental National News Council was established as a monitor of accuracy and fairness of news reporting.

TYPES OF CRITICISM

The criticism was not surprising, given the nature of modern times. In a democratic, consumer-oriented, technological society that is increasingly dependent on exchange of information, the news media have become an all-pervasive, powerful force. They speak to, for, and about all people, and Americans rely on them for information essential to ordered living. Yet, it is impossible to satisfy everyone in a dynamic, heterogeneous society.

To perform their public-service function and still remain free of government regulation, the media are commercial enterprises in business to make money. In an "age of information," they are impelled toward consolidation and centralized control by the economies inherent in bigness and standardization. Their need for mass audiences to ensure income from advertising normally leads them to seek the lowest common denominator in appeal.

The news system's own technological advancement has made its role more complex and ubiquitous. Improved techniques for gathering and transmitting news have expanded the availability of "knowable" information for which Americans seem to have no end of desire. Thus, the media's role is not only more powerful than ever before, but also more visible and vulnerable.

Strangely, while the press sees itself as an adversary of the "establishment," the public tends to see the press as part of the "establishment." And although polls have indicated a "credibility gap" between the press and the public, there is no clear manifestation of hostility among the general public. Criticism of the news media comes largely from opinion leaders such as government officials, politicians, businessmen, and other members of the "establishment." It is from these sectors that threats to First Amendment freedoms, however effective thus far, have come: wiretaps on journalists and attempts to cut off leaks from government; "gag" orders and other court-imposed restrictions on the reporting of trials; subpoenas that force journalists to testify in legal proceedings; efforts to force journalists to reveal their sources.

Centralized Control. There are two aspects of the issue of centralized control of the news media. One is the concentration of major, influential outlets in what critics call the New York–Washington "liberal axis"; the other is the consolidation of newspapers and broadcast stations into chains and conglomerates.

Attention on the first aspect hit its peak during the Nixon administration's campaign against what it considered a hostile press. Spiro Agnew, then Vice President, struck the keynote when he attacked television news in a 1969 speech:

> A small group of men, numbering perhaps no more than a dozen, decide what 40 to 50 million Americans will learn of the day's events in the nation and the world. . . . To a man these commentators and producers live and work in the geographical and intellectual confines of Washington, D.C., or New York City. . . . They draw their political and social views from the same sources. Worse, they talk constantly to one another, thereby providing artificial reinforcement to their shared viewpoints.

Agnew was referring to the fact that the newscasts of the three major networks, which are seen on the average by at least 40 million Americans each night, emanate from Washington and New York, where the networks have their headquarters. In addition to the networks, talk of a "liberal axis" generally means the *New York Times* and the *Washington Post*, and *Time* and *Newsweek*. While these voices often agree in their views, including criticism of the Nixon administration concerning Watergate, they cannot be regarded as unanimous on all subjects.

Still, because these voices are located in the political and communications capitals of the country, they exert editorial power not found elsewhere. They set the editorial lead and tone for many other newspapers as well as the New York–based wire services. In an analysis of journalism since 1960, *Fortune* magazine concluded that the news media and their audiences, once sharply decentralized, had added a national dimension.[1]

Consolidation has increased concern about a diminution of diversity in information available to the public. Mergers of newspapers, along with the deaths of others, has meant a loss of competitive voices in most cities. Critics contend that once-independent newspapers and broadcast stations have been purchased by chain ownerships which often impose common policies and viewpoints on their members. Many news outlets have been absorbed into industrial conglomerates whose principal interests are not news communications.

Defenders of consolidation argue that chain ownership can enhance the strength, independence, and diversity of individual papers and stations. They say that corporate membership has the advantage of efficient management, strong capitalization, national recruiting of talent, and financial support for First Amendment challenges. Al Neuharth, president and chief executive of the Gannett Company, a leading newspaper chain, told an editors' convention in 1977 that who owns newspapers is not nearly as important as what the owners do with them.[2]

Conformity. Related to centralized control is the question of conformity of news. The news system as a whole tends to adhere to a standardized pattern based largely on follow the leader. As a result, newspapers and newscasts on any day are similar in content—despite the fact that there are hundreds of news items to choose from.

Conformity is most prominent in national and international news. The reason is that virtually all newspapers and broadcast stations, unable to afford their own correspondents in faraway places, rely on the wire services for their national and international stories. The stories available for use are those that the press association editors in New York choose to put on the wires. And these editors are greatly influenced by the choices made by the prestigious newspapers and broadcast networks in New York and Washington.

Similarly, broadcast tends to follow print in the selection of news to pass on. Broadcast news departments do not have the manpower to do much original reporting, so they look to the newspapers and wire services for their leads. Thus, the network newscasts closely resemble the front pages of the *New York Times* and the *Washington Post*, and the local station's local report resembles the front page of the local newspaper. Conformity is further accentuated by the increasing use of stories distributed by the *New York Times* News Service and similar "supplemental" wire services, and "canned" editorials and features bought from syndicates by small papers and stations.

A part of the conformity issue is a widely criticized practice known as "pack reporting." Instead of seeking out the news independently, some competing reporters, perhaps either lazy under deadline pressure or afraid of being "scooped," follow each other after the news. Pack reporters usually end up with the same stories and thus add to the conformity of news presented to the public.

Bias and Access. Criticism of centralized control also includes complaints about bias and limited access.

The press traditionally has been accused of reflecting the bias of its owners and, as big business itself, usually the viewpoints of big business and the "establishment." Although an anti-establishment trend developed in the late 1960s and early 1970s, critics point out that the media are dependent for revenue on advertising from businesses; and they contend that, since businesses function best in a calm environment, the media have an imperative to support the status quo against change.

This imperative, the critics say, works against minorities and the deprived who seek change. Further, the critics argue that the minorities and deprived have no guaranteed outlet for their views because the media, as private enterprises, control the use of their newspaper columns and broadcast programs. The restricted access also means that there is no dependable recourse for timely reply by those who believe they have been misused, or wronged through distortion or inaccuracy, in news stories.

Managed News. Another criticism is that the news media often give too much emphasis to predictable, or "arranged," news from established institutions. This news may grow out of a scheduled press conference, a "staged" event such as an official's inspection tour of a slum, or an announcement by an important organization such as the Defense Department or General Motors. Critics contend that reporters sometimes accept the situation at face value, without trying to "get behind" the obvious events.

In such situations, the critics say, there is the tendency for some reporters to adopt the bias and language of the organization that arranged the event or made the announcement. And this, the *Fortune* analysis pointed out, makes it possible for the organization to "manipulate—and distort—the citizen's impression of the way things are."[3] Moreover, critics say, an emphasis on information from institutional sources can mean underrepresentation in the news for groups not represented by an important organization.

Power Abuse. Starting in the 1960s, and intensifying during the Watergate crisis, an apparent switch in attitude from proestablishment to antiestablishment drew criticism to some sectors of the media. The change coincided with the emergence of advocacy journalism and "new" journalism characterized by subjective reporting. Overzealousness in investigations and attacks on institutions and individuals brought charges that the news media were abusing their power.

The *Fortune* analysis pointed out that the trend in the press was influenced by new currents in American life:

> A new generation of Americans—better educated, more interested in ideas, more concerned with political and social questions—gave many institutions a more "intellectual" character in the 1960s. It had a crucial impact on the new national newspapers, which were developing new journalistic forms; furthermore, the national press as a whole seemed to have a new consciousness of American society and was conveying a new and more "serious" agenda to the American people.[4]

It was during this period that the news media began to add more interpretation to their recording of events. They focused less on events and more on ideas, trends, and causes, such as the civil-rights and antiwar movements. News became politicized, with emphasis on adversary investigations. The result of all this was conditions conducive to differing interpretations and disagreements.

The aftermath of the Watergate investigations brought charges of excesses on the part of the press. While no one denied that adversary journalism was essential in a democracy, there was new stress on the need for accuracy, thoroughness, and responsibility in investigations. John A. Scali of ABC News, who served as a United States representative to the United Nations, typified the view that post-Watergate journalism was in danger of losing its perspective.

"The pendulum has swung too far in the journalistic zeal to

rout out evil," he said in a 1976 speech. "There is almost a tendency not to treat the government as an adversary, but as an enemy."[5]

Katharine Graham, chairman of the board of the Washington Post Company, whose newspaper was a leader in the media investigations of Watergate, said in discussing probes of public officials: "An emphasis on candor and an absence of wrongdoing, although primary and vital, can distort the process of assessment if it is carried to extremes and distracts the public and the press from other, equally significant questions."[6]

A central point in the criticism was that the press was fostering a systematic distrust of all established institutions and that such distrust hindered the conduct of the public's government and economic business. Pointing to Walter Lippmann's thesis that a key role of journalism was to facilitate transactions between institutions, critics contended that an antiestablishment attitude on the part of the press made it difficult for government, business, and other institutions to explain themselves to their publics.

Crisis Journalism. Despite the trend toward more in-depth treatment of news and interpretation, some critics maintain that the news media still are crisis-oriented. Charles Seib, ombudsman at the *Washington Post*, refers to "the dailiness that makes news coverage distorted and shallow" and concludes, "We're still geared to the banner headline and gee-whiz approach."

Roger Wilkins, who specializes in urban affairs for the *New York Times*, told a group of journalism students in 1976 that the press is "good at covering crises, but we go into a slump on day-to-day coverage." Referring to coverage of the governmental process, he said, "We report appointments, decisions, and problems, but not what happens in-between."

Even Watergate, which resulted in plaudits for the press for its enterprise, has been cited as evidence of journalism's weakness in monitoring governmental activities over the long run. "Watergate showed how ineffective the press is in protecting us from excesses such as those of the Nixon Administration," syndicated columnist Garry Wills has said.

The preoccupation with crises, many critics contend, results in inadequate detection and coverage of more significant developments. Usually included in the catalog of issues "overlooked"

until "discovered" by independent investigators are the threat
of chemical pesticides, the lack of consumer protection, the
developing civil-rights movement, the hunger problem, and the
energy shortage.

"Hunger in America is hardly remembered," Lewis W. Wolf-
son, a former Washington correspondent turned journalism professor, wrote in 1976. "Civil rights? Busing is front-page news,
but the larger struggle for minority rights is victim to the press's
short attention span."[7]

Thus, many critics believe that the press must put more stress
on investigative reporting in areas far less obvious than the
Watergate abuses, and on explanations of complicated issues in
an increasingly baffling world. For this, the media need more
expertise in many fields to enable them to lay out alternative
options and possible solutions to problems facing society.

Sex, Violence, and Trivia. Along with the crisis syndrome, the
press draws criticism for its emphasis on sex, violence, and trivia.

Sex and violence have always titillated people; they have been
media staples since the days of the penny press and "yellow
journalism." Editors therefore spotlight stories on these subjects
to attract audiences. In the mid-1970s there was heavy stress on
gossip and scandal. The trouble, say critics, is that these stories
often displace stories about more significant issues.

A case in point has been cited by reporter James V. Risser of
the *Des Moines Register and Tribune.* Writing in 1976, Risser
noted that the newspapers and newscasts were reporting in detail
the affair of Representative Wayne Hays and Elizabeth Ray, a
woman on the congressional payroll. At the same time, said
Risser, the media, except for his paper, were ignoring a
multimillion-dollar export grain scandal.[8] It was only after Congress began investigating the alleged corruption, and a few other
newspapers started their own inquiries, that the story got some
national coverage.

Trivia can include just about anything, from panty raids to
a movie starlet's new hairdo, but the kind that provokes most
serious criticism characterized coverage of the 1976 presidential
race between Jimmy Carter and Gerald Ford. The news that got
the biggest headlines concerned a Carter remark about ethnic
purity, a Carter interview with *Playboy* magazine, a Ford mis-

statement about Eastern Europe, and questions about Ford's finances. Virtually ignored were policy questions related to such national issues as acute inflation, severe unemployment, and the energy problem.

While the candidates were partly to blame because they played down substantive issues in their oratory, some critics also blamed the nature of the news system. In a *New York Times* analysis, Joseph Lelyveld noted an argument advanced by some academic observers of political campaigns: "The candidates, it is argued, have to adapt themselves to the structure of the communications system. The electronic era, so the argument goes, puts a premium on pithy 25-second answers and, as a result, there is a built-in tendency to downplay substantive political differences."[9]

Ethics. Within the context of the broad areas discussed above there are many ethical violations which, when they occur, justify criticism of the offending media. Norman Isaacs, a veteran newspaper executive and journalism professor who has served as chairman of the National News Council, uses the following list when discussing ethics with journalism students:

> major inaccuracies; willful slanting; prejudicial editing; misuse of photographs; artificial posing of pictures; suppression of news; use of news space for puffery; a refusal to correct errors and attempts to hide them; secret taping of conversations; violation of legal rights; invasion of privacy; cover-up of conflict of interest; racial and national stereotypes; lapses in taste; manipulation of quotes out of context; acceptance of arranged or doctored news.

MONITORS OF THE MEDIA

Faced with widespread criticism and moves against their freedoms, the news media in recent years have begun, however slowly, to change their traditional "self-righteous" attitude against self-examination and reform.

At least a score of newspapers have created positions of ombudsmen and media critics. Ombudsmen generally comment on coverage by their own papers and deal with public complaints about the coverage; media critics examine and criticize the behavior of the news media as a whole. In most cases, the ombudsmen and critics are independent from the rest of their staffs and operate without interference from management.

Several magazines, including *Time* and *Esquire,* have media columns with commentary about the news system. The magazine [*More*], the *Columbia Journalism Review,* the *Washington Journalism Review,* and several similar publications have been devoted entirely to activities of the media. A scattering of broadcast programs include commentaries on the media.

In 1973, after years of debate about its need, the National News Council was created as an independent monitor of national press problems. Organized by a task force under the aegis of the Twentieth Century Fund, it is financed largely by media-oriented groups.

The council's stated purpose is "to receive, to examine, and to report on complaints concerning the accuracy and fairness of news reporting in the United States, as well as to initiate studies and report on issues involving the freedom of the press." The council limited its jurisdiction to what the task force called "the principal national suppliers of news."

The council has no enforcement power. It relies on publicity given complaints and council recommendations to generate moral force for remedies. Executive director William Arthur has said that by acting as "a forum for ventilation of grievances," the council serves as "a buffer against governmental encroachment and regulation."

A major obstacle to effectiveness is that the concept and operation of the council are not backed by some major suppliers of news, including Associated Press, United Press International, the *New York Times,* the *Washington Post,* and the Newhouse News Service. Arthur Ochs Sulzberger, publisher of the *Times,* said that readers should be the ultimate judges of a newspaper's fairness and accuracy, and that the *Times* does not want one organization to act as "investigator, prosecutor, and judge rolled into one."

Behind the active monitors are the respected standards of professional journalism. They are set out in the Canons of Journalism of the American Society of Newspaper Editors, the Code of Broadcast News Ethics of the Radio Television News Directors Association, and the Basic Statement of Principles of the National Conference of Editorial Writers.

NOTES

1. *Fortune*, April 1975, p. 122.
2. *Bulletin* of the American Society of Newspaper Editors, May/June 1977, p. 6.
3. *Fortune*, p. 123.
4. *Ibid.*, p. 122.
5. *New York Times*, March 29, 1976, p. 28.
6. *New York Times*, Dec. 2, 1974, p. 17.
7. *Quill*, Nov. 1976, p. 20.
8. *Bulletin* of the American Society of Newspaper Editors, Sept. 1976, p. 17.
9. *New York Times*, Nov. 1, 1976, p. 39.

SUGGESTED READING

Bagdikian, Ben H. *The Effete Conspiracy and Other Crimes by the Press.* New York: Harper and Row, 1972.

Boorstein, Daniel J. *The Image or What Happened to the American Dream.* New York: Atheneum, 1962.

Epstein, Edward J. *News from Nowhere.* New York: Random House, 1973.

Hohenberg, John. *The News Media: A Journalist Looks at His Profession.* New York: Holt, Rinehart & Winston, Inc., 1968.

Seiden, Martin H. *Who Controls the Mass Media?* New York: Basic Books, 1974.

7
A Look Ahead

By the 1970s, it was clear that the world was entering the "Information Age." Information was proliferating as a result of a communications revolution that had profound implications for the mass media—and, indeed, for the lives of all people. For the future, new technology, such as cable television, promises vast changes in the ways that people receive news and exchange ideas. Visionaries foresee the day when homes will have communications centers that combine all the media.

The prospect poses new challenges. With the growing complexity of society, information is essential to the proper use of resources and smooth functioning of institutions. Knowledge is power. Thus, it is important that the public understands the new "information machines" and recognizes the need for distribution of control over them.

THE TECHNOLOGY

Computers are already revolutionizing the newsrooms and composing rooms of newspapers, which had remained fundamentally unchanged since the invention of the linotype machine nearly a century ago. Cables and satellites are expanding the capabilities of television. In the wings are such advances as fiber optics communications, which are expected to improve the transmission of information greatly at lower cost than present methods.

Computers. Pencils, typewriters, and paper are rapidly being replaced by computers and televisionlike consoles in the nation's newspaper offices. Data banks and retrieval systems are replacing library "morgues" of newspaper clippings and other research information. Computerized machines are replacing the manual typesetting equipment in composing rooms where newspaper stories are transformed into print. The result of this automation is a vast saving in time and manpower, and consequently cost, involved in the gathering, transmission, and production of news.

The major wire services, AP and UPI, have been using the computer-console systems since the early 1970s and anticipate further transmission improvements. At least half the nation's newspapers have automated to some degree, and most of the rest are in the processing of doing so.

With the new system, the reporter types on a keyboard of the terminal console, and his story appears on a screen above, rather than on paper. The story goes into a computer, along with other stories, for processing into print. Editing and other changes are accomplished in the same way.

On the horizon are light portable keyboards, which reporters in the field will be able to use to transmit information via radio, telephone, or portable facsimile machines, and computerized systems for making up newspaper pages on terminal screens. When an entire page is laid out on a terminal, a high-speed phototypesetter will take just minutes to retrieve the designated stories from the computer's memory and turn out a fully assembled page.

Aside from reducing costs, the automated system gives editorial people more control over the finished product (because it eliminates manual steps in the composing room); it reduces the time between story deadlines and press runs, which means the printed news is fresher; and it provides a newspaper with more flexibility for new editions or sections directed at specific audiences (such as certain suburban areas).

Cable TV. If newspaper computerization reaches the level that all information is in digital form, the information could be transmitted electronically to the home. This would mean a teaming up of the newspaper operation and cable TV to produce a newspaper on the home TV screen. Such information probably would be limited to headlines, stock-market quotations, movie listings, weather, and the like; and longer newspaper articles, analyses, and other material for rereading or keeping would continue in printed newspaper form. Experimental home information services have been tried in England and Japan.

Cable TV, with its multichannel capacity, has the potential for more diversity of information, including educational and medical services. Because it can be directed at specific audiences, it can be used for activities of local organizations and minority groups that do not have access to commercial TV.

Although the costs are still high, cable TV also has the potential for two-way communications, which would allow the viewer to order specific information on the screen by pushing a button. Ultimately, if developed fully, cable TV is seen as the basis for the long-heralded "wired city" concept.

Satellites. Space satellites, which have made simultaneous, instantaneous global communications a reality, have the potential for direct broadcast that would eliminate local facilities. This would open up enormous social and educational possibilities for many developing nations that cannot afford conventional TV broadcast stations. In the United States, satellites also could be used to pick up signals from a local over-the-air TV station and distribute the signals to cable systems around the country.

Another future use of satellites for news purposes is the transmission of facsimiles of newspaper and magazine pages. The process enables nationally circulated publications to print and distribute their products simultaneously in different parts of the country.

Fiber Optics. One of the most significant technological advances is fiber optics, seen as an eventual replacement for coaxial cable for transmission of information. Fiber optics deals with the transmission of light and images (as around bends and curves) through a flexible bundle of plastic optical fibers. This type of transmission is lighter and smaller than coaxial cable, and is expected eventually to have more capability at lower cost. The predicted uses for fiber optics include two-way television and two-way teletype services.

THE EFFECTS

The new technology undoubtedly will alter the roles and patterns, including advertising, of the mass media and give the individual more choice in what he wants to read or watch. While the emphasis may be swinging toward broadcasting, it is not likely that the printed media will die out. Newspapers, magazines, and books satisfy the intellectual curiosity for browsing, for permanent records, for details and interpretation.

Nevertheless, there is likely to be less distinction between the various media as home information services develop. Cable TV will bring to the home screen much of the information now found in newspapers, magazines, and books. With transmission easier and quicker, information will come from more sources than ever before, and videotaping will permit viewing at leisure. At the same time, information will be less centralized and receivers of information will be increasingly fragmented because the new technology will enable the media to direct their messages at narrower audiences.

How it all may come together in a home communications center has been forecast by David Sarnoff of Radio Corporation of America:

> Today's console and table model furniture may be displaced by an all-purpose television screen, mounted on the wall. It would be coupled to a sound system and a high-speed electronic printer for recording any information the viewer wishes to retain.
>
> This means that the major channel of news, information, and entertainment in the home will be a single integrated system that combines all of the separate electronic instruments and printed means of communications today—television set, radio, newspaper, magazine, and book.
>
> The home will thus be joined to a new, all-embracing information medium with a global reach. This medium will serve a vast public of differing nationalities, languages, and customs and its import will be profound.[1]

THE CHALLENGE

As the new technology develops, the mass media will become more efficient, capable of collecting larger reservoirs of information than ever before. The potential for creating ideas and images will be unprecedented. Therefore, how the media are controlled and the information is used could go a long way toward determining the shape of society in the future.

Today the media, especially television, are largely centralized, are controlled by a relatively few people, and offer only limited access to the public. The news systems are highly selective and are geared to commercial marketing. Tomorrow's systems will provide not only news but also basic informational services essential for everyday living. With cable TV as the basis, there will be many channels for information and exchange of ideas, at the local level not now available. It is essential, therefore, that consideration be given to the accessibility of the channels to the general public.

Another factor, as Ben Bagdikian points out in *The Information Machines*, is the probable disparity of ownership of home communications centers. The home cable connected with a computer eventually will be as important to urban man as the telephone in carrying out his daily business, Bagdikian notes, but a home communications system could be too expensive for the poor.

"Consequently, public policy needs to encourage the spreading of new devices with equity throughout the population, as educational devices and as methods of dealing effectively with the outside environment," Bagdikian asserts. "Otherwise, the new information machines could create semi-permanent class divisions and widen an already dangerous chasm between social groups who see the same environment in incompatible ways."[2]

NOTES

1. William L. Rivers, Theodore Peterson and Jay W. Jensen, *The Mass Media and Modern Society* (San Francisco: Rinehart Press, 1971), p. 322.
2. Ben H. Bagdikian, *The Information Machines* (New York: Harper Colophon Books, 1971), p. 281.

SUGGESTED READING

Bagdikian, Ben H. *The Information Machines*. New York: Harper Colophon Books, 1971.

8

How the News Teams
Are Organized

Translating the events and issues of the day—from muggings to diplomatic meetings—into an interesting and informative news report requires the skills and teamwork of a variety of journalists. The newspaper manpower pattern, which is the prevailing model for all the media, has three basic parts: the managerial editors, the reporters, and the copy editors and other news processors.

Because of the mechanical complexities of producing a newspaper or newscast, and the time pressures to "get the news out," the editorial process demands careful planning within a scrupulous routine. Delegation of authority, trust, and cooperation are essential.

The manpower pattern and work routine are fairly standardized, and apply generally to the wire services, broadcast stations, and newsmagazines as well as the newspapers. There are variations, of course: no two news organizations do things exactly alike, and the size and makeup of the editorial staff depend largely on the size of the organization. The number of news personnel can range from two or three on a rural weekly to nine hundred on the *New York Times*.

THE PUBLISHER

At the top of a newspaper's power pyramid is the publisher—the owner or his representative. The publisher is the newspaper's chief executive, with ultimate authority over the five departments: editorial, production, mechanical, circulation, and business. On smaller papers, the publisher may play an active role in the day-to-day editorial operations; on larger papers, because of the pressures of time and space, he usually delegates executive authority to his top editors and devotes himself to overall policy matters. Whatever the case, the publisher makes the final decisions and determines the general direction his newspaper will take.

MANAGERIAL EDITORS

Putting out a newspaper every day requires advance planning, intelligent organization of manpower, efficient coordination of interdependent activities. It involves a continuous succession of crucial judgments and quick decisions. Except on the smallest of papers, where the process is quantitatively limited, one person cannot possibly handle all the details of gathering, selecting, processing, and publishing the news.

The typical news organization has managerial editors, headed by the managing editor, who supervise and direct various aspects of the editorial operation ("editorial" applies to information that is not advertising). These editors determine which news will be covered and included in the day's report to the public. While they are fewer than the reporters and news processors, they exert more influence on the overall product.

The pattern described here is for a large paper; it is not the only pattern, but it is typical of most. On small papers some of the jobs are combined.

Managing Editor. Although some newspapers have editors-in-chief or executive editors, in most cases the managing editor is the captain of the news team. He is the overall supervisor of news coverage and is responsible for getting out the paper. He is the driving force, the standard setter, and the paper usually reflects his ideas and character. Concerned primarily with the "big picture," the managing editor delegates the detail work to his lieutenants.

To meet his responsibilities, the managing editor must be up-to-the-minute on what is happening in his community and in the world. He must know the capabilities of his reporters and editors so that he can make proper assignments. He must understand the logistical vagaries of gathering news quickly in strange places, sometimes in foreign lands. He must delegate authority intelligently and orchestrate the teamwork sensitively. He must think and act fast under pressure from all sides. He must be continually aware of the flow of news copy, although he usually has an assistant managing editor or news editor to help him with this important task.

City Editor. Among the most active of the supervisors, the city editor directs the local reporters who provide the biggest chunk of news in the newspaper. Since most of the newspaper's readers are local residents, and the paper's business life is sustained by the community in which it operates, local news must be covered in detail. The city editor must have his finger on the community's pulse at all times. He must maintain channels to community officials and businessmen. He must anticipate expected news as well as prepare for unexpected events.

The city editor assigns the stories and deploys his corps of reporters so that the major news of the day is adequately covered. He oversees the assignments while in progress, and reviews the resultant stories before they go into print. In recent years, because local coverage has spilled into the suburbs, city editors on some large papers have become metropolitan editors.

National and Foreign Editors. News from outside the local region is supervised by national and foreign editors. On large metropolitan papers that have staffs of correspondents the functions are separate; on smaller papers they may be combined and handled by one person. The national, or telegraph, editor deals with correspondents in Washington and elsewhere in the United States. The foreign, or cable, editor does the same with correspondents overseas.

Removed from the scenes of action, national and foreign editors can give orders or advice only by telephone, telegraph, or cable messages from the home office. If the newspaper has no correspondents, the national/foreign editors' function is to deal with the national and international news stories received on wire-service machines. Every daily subscribes to at least one wire service; large papers subscribe to both AP and UPI and perhaps a few supplementary services.

Department Editors. Every newspaper of any size has a sports department and culture/entertainment department. Most larger newspapers now have separate business/finance and lifestyle departments. There may even be a travel department and a real estate department. These departments are supervised by department editors who make the assignments and oversee the coverage. In some cases the department editors are responsible to the city editor; in others, to the managing editor.

Editorial-Page Editor. The editorial page and other views and opinion pages are the responsibility of a special editor. Whatever his title, this editor works with editorial writers, columnists, and special feature writers who contribute to these pages. The editorial-page editor generally answers to the publisher and has no formal relationship with the news department.

REPORTERS

Of all newspaper editorial personnel, reporters are the most visible and numerous. They are the front line of the newsgathering process. On large newspapers, the number of reporters may range from a dozen to a hundred; on small dailies, there may be only three or four. Reporters fall into three broad categories: "beat," general assignment, and special assignment.

Beat reporters have fixed daily assignments at places such as city hall, the courts, and police stations where news ordinarily originates. General-assignment reporters handle straight-news stories that do not originate on beats. Special-assignment reporters concentrate on special fields of interest such as sports, legal affairs, science, and religion.

On a metropolitan newspaper the reporter functions are defined quite clearly, although "beats" may vary according to the size of the staff and community. A reporter on the police beat may also check on the airports and incoming ships. The city hall reporter may also have responsibility for the hotels and other public buildings in the downtown area.

On a small paper, a reporter usually is a beat/generalist/ specialist combination who covers five or six stories in a day. He may make the rounds of city hall, the court building, and police and fire headquarters in the morning; cover a Rotary Club lunch speaker at noon; dash off to a fire or feature interview in the afternoon; and end up with the high school basketball game in the evening.

NEWS PROCESSORS

Once a news story is written by the reporter, it goes to "inside" deskpersons who put it in shape for final printing. They give it a headline, determine its length, and decide where it will be placed in the paper.

Copy Editors. The copy editor is the guardian of the news-paper's content and how it looks in print. He is the final check-point between reporter and public. In their book *Headlines and Deadlines*, Robert E. Garst and Theodore M. Bernstein describe the desired qualities of a copy editor:

> The ideal copy editor not only would have a complete mastery over the technical phases of his work, such as the editing of copy and the writing of headlines, but would possess sound and swift judgment, would be an expert rhetorician and grammarian and would be thor-oughly versed in government, politics, astrophysics, home gardening, shoes, ships, sealing wax and all subjects that find or are likely to find a place in the kaleidoscopic enterprise that is the modern newspaper.[1]

Editing the copy and writing headlines are the copy editor's main functions. In editing the copy, he checks for accuracy and eliminates any errors; corrects the grammar and adjusts the language to the paper's standardized style; polishes the writing and makes sure the content is in true perspective and not libelous; trims excessive verbiage and tailors the story length to fit the allotted space. In writing the headline, the copy editor captures the essence of the news in title form designed to entice the reader into examining the full story.

Newspaper myth pictures the copy editor as the "enemy" of the reporter, a mutilator of good copy. In reality, the experienced reporter regards the experienced copy editor as a friendly and constructive critic who can improve the copy and protect him, as well as the paper, from blunders.

Rewriters. Journalists with a talent for fast and facile writing often are assigned to write stories based on information phoned in by reporters. When the reporter who wrote the original story is not available, the rewrite person also may be asked to "rework" a story that needs revision or updating as deadline approaches.

Researchers. Many large news organizations have researchers, either in the newsroom or in charge of the "morgue," where the "dead" news of the past is stored. Today's news often flows from yesterday's, and the role of the researchers is to provide the writers with facts and background material that will put today's news in proper perspective.

Layout Editors. The placement of stories on pages, their lengths, and the overall typographical appearance of the newspaper are the concerns of the layout editor. The number and lengths of stories to be included are determined by the amount of advertising matter for the day and the number of columns allotted to news. In consultation with the top editors, the layout editor works out the best arrangement of stories and headlines on "dummy" pages, and then acts as liaison between the newsroom and the composing room as the finished pages are prepared for printing.

THE DAILY ROUTINE

The work of the editorial department must be coordinated closely with the work of the advertising, mechanical, and circulation departments. Deadlines must be met throughout the day if the newspaper is to be ready for delivery at the time the consumer, through habit, expects it. This means that the editors and reporters must adhere to a rigid schedule and constantly plan ahead.

Although the basic routine is similar on all newspapers, there is some difference between afternoon and morning papers. The afternoon paper is put together as the news develops during the day, which means considerable change and updating of stories. The morning paper is compiled after most of the news-producing events take place, and the operation thus is more stable. The afternoon operation is more typical in the United States because there are more than four times as many P.M. papers as A.M.

Most large dailies have a "dayside" staff and a "nightside" staff. Generally speaking, the dayside gathers or directs the gathering of the news, and the nightside edits the news and puts the paper together. On smaller papers, one staff does it all, usually in a shorter time frame than on large papers.

The day begins with the editors' review of scheduled news events, such as press conferences and meetings, and of situations that have developed overnight, such as a flood or a government crisis. The editors evaluate the many news possibilities, decide on priorities for coverage, and assign reporters to specific stories.

Throughout the day the reporters keep in telephone contact with their editors, alerting them to developments in the assigned stories and also to potential stories of spontaneous origin that they may have come across. As the reports come in, the editors constantly adjust their story priorities and operating plan.

By afternoon, the reporters return to the office to write their stories. In cases of late-breaking stories, the reporters may phone in information to rewriters. The finished stories are checked by the city, national, and foreign editors, and then are sent to the copy desk for editing and headlines. In the meantime, the top editors select the stories they want to include in the paper, and decide how the stories should be laid out in the pages. The completed stories and headlines, tailored to fit the page layouts, are then sent to the composing room for setting in type, and finally to the press room for printing.

THE WIRE SERVICES

The newsgathering system of the wire services is similar in many ways to the newspaper system, and different in others. The wire services have central news rooms in New York where the managerial editors plan and direct coverage, and copy editors and rewriters process copy that comes in. The services also station reporters in centers of significant news activity.

Where the two systems differ is in the emphasis and scope of the coverage, and the deployment of reporters. Newspapers are concerned primarily with news of their local areas; the wire services are concerned primarily with news of general interest to clients in many places. Thus, the wire services do not maintain large teams of reporters in any one place, except for Washington.

To gather the general-interest news, the wire services have bureaus in most major cities in the United States and in capitals abroad. Small staffs of reporters working out of the bureaus cover significant events in their areas and channel their stories into headquarters and other bureaus via teletype. At various relay points, the stories go through a process of selection, editing, and redistribution to suit the needs of newspaper and broadcast clients in specific regions.

BROADCAST NEWS

The broadcast news operation is patterned after that of the newspaper, but scaled down in both manpower and activity. For radio and television, news is secondary to entertainment. The newsgathering techniques are modified to take advantage of the audiovisual dimension of broadcast.

Radio. Although radio stations have frequent newscasts throughout the day, the total amount of news they deliver is much less than in the average newspaper. Because newscasts are brief, few stories can be included and each story is presented in headline form. Many of the same stories are repeated on successive newscasts.

Radio news departments, at stations that have them, have a news director who makes the assignments, selects the news to be aired, and generally supervises the operation. The larger stations have reporters, editors, and writers to gather and process the news, and "airmen" who present the news on the air. Because of the emphasis on speed, telephone reporting is common for local coverage, and tape-recorded playbacks add immediacy to the stories. National and international news generally comes from a wire service machine.

Some small stations concentrate on local news, but most do not have sufficient manpower and their newscasts consist mainly of "rip and read" reports from the wire service machine.

Television. The organization of TV news operations is the same as that of radio operations, but television generally has fewer news programs each day. The major emphasis in TV news is at the network level.

Network news departments are large and talented, including Washington and foreign correspondents and highly paid anchorpersons. As a result, the evening newscasts are elaborate affairs, although still a headline service compared with newspapers.

The factor that sets TV news operations apart is the need for pictures. This means that much expense and manpower are devoted to getting film crews to news events, and reporting must be reconciled with the availability of good, usable pictures.

NEWSMAGAZINES

Newsmagazines are published weekly and are aimed at general national and international audiences. Therefore, they are not concerned with local news coverage as are newspapers and broadcast stations. Although the editorial personnel and activities are similar to those of a newspaper, the reporters are scattered around the world rather than concentrated locally.

The distinguishing aspect of the newsmagazine operation is the practice of "group journalism" (or more irreverently, "journalism by committee"). Under this system, most stories are the result of work by many reporters, researchers, writers, and editors. Information comes into the central newsroom from all directions, is sifted and refined, and finally written and rewritten in final form under the watchful eyes of the managerial editors.

NOTES

1. Robert E. Garth and Theodore M. Bernstein, *Headlines and Deadlines* (New York: Columbia University Press, 1961), p. vii.

SUGGESTED READING

Garth, Robert E., and Bernstein, Theodore M. *Headlines and Deadlines.* New York: Columbia University Press, 1961.
Hohenberg, John. *The Professional Journalist.* New York: Holt, Rinehart and Winston, Inc., 1969.

9

How the News Is Gathered

Gathering the news is the central function of journalism; all else in the news process—writing, editing, interpreting, presenting—flows from it. Some news can be anticipated, other news cannot. It is the job of the managerial editors to monitor the flow of news and to arrange the coverage by observing events and by communicating with sources of information, be they people or written material. The reporter traditionally has been guided by two axioms: The story is only as good as the information gathered for it; and the reporter is no better than his or her sources.

Although their assignments may differ widely, all reporters face common challenges and follow similar procedures. All, too, must abide by certain legal restraints in their pursuit of news. Most news is gathered by the general-assignment and "beat" reporters, but in recent years the subject specialist and the probing investigator have enlarged their roles.

TYPES OF NEWS

While news events are as diverse as life itself, they fall into two basic categories as far as journalists are concerned. Some events can be anticipated, and thus can be prepared for; others originate spontaneously, and thus can disrupt well-laid plans.

Anticipated news flows from events that are scheduled in advance: a City Council meeting, the opening of a murder trial, a symposium at the university, a concert by a touring singer, a news conference to announce a new consumer product, a baseball game. On an ordinary day these kinds of events make up the bulk of the news.

Anticipated news is convenient to gather. Since editors know that these events are almost sure to happen, they can make arrangements in advance to cover them and can plan their daily news reports accordingly. A reporter assigned to cover the events knows that they will take place at specified times, usually with known casts of characters, usually with familiar patterns, often with predictable results.

News that cannot be anticipated relates mainly to disasters: natural calamities such as floods and earthquakes, and unexpected events such as fires, highway accidents, and burglaries. There are also news conferences that are not announced in advance, sudden developments in business or diplomatic negotiations, surprise discoveries in scientific research. Although editors cannot anticipate such events, they must be prepared to cover them when they occur and adjust their overall newsgathering plans accordingly.

KEEPING ON TOP OF THE NEWS

The managerial editors are responsible for deciding which events and issues should be covered by their limited reportorial staffs. Because newsgathering is a continuous process and involves periodic deadlines, the editors try to anticipate the news as much as possible. At the same time, because all news obviously cannot be anticipated, the editors have reporters deployed strategically "in the field" watching for the unexpected.

Editors stay "on top of the news" in many ways. They maintain "futures" books with listings of events scheduled in advance. They contact community leaders regularly to check on "what's new" in a department, a civic organization, a labor union. They receive friendly tips from "informed sources." They peruse the steady stream of public-relations announcements about developments in virtually every field and institutional activity. They monitor the press association wires and their competitors' operations. They keep in touch with their reporters at city hall or police headquarters, or roaming the community on general assignment.

Armed with this accumulated information, and research material that fills in the gaps, the editors systematically piece together their newsgathering plans every day. Starting with the anticipated events and adjusting as the unanticipated ones develop, the editors evaluate all the news possibilities, decide which are the most important, and assign coverage accordingly.

The key person in the local newsgathering operation is the city editor, and the key organizational tool is the assignment sheet. The city editor assigns specific reporters to specific stories, consults with the reporters as the stories develop, and assesses the significance and proper writing of the stories. On the assignment sheet, the city editor designates the stories being covered, the names of the reporters assigned to them, and usually the times the stories are expected to be completed. Thus, with a glance at the sheet, the city editor knows immediately the disposition of all reporters under his supervision, and the gathering momentum of the day's news.

The routine is similar for national and foreign coverage in news organizations large enough to have correspondents in addition to local reporters. The national and foreign editors assign the stories to their respective correspondents, keeping a chart of the coverage in progress.

OBSERVATION AND SOURCES

The task of the newsgatherer is the search for truth, or as Lincoln Steffens, noted journalist of the muckraking era, put it, "the letting in of light and air." In pursuing the search, the reporter relies on his own personal observations and on consultation with sources that can augment his observations.

Direct observation is the best method of obtaining information. The alert and intelligent reporter tries every means to be on the scene of an event: to see firemen fighting a blaze, to hear the mayor make a statement, to "feel" the mood at a protest demonstration. The reporter knows that information acquired from direct observation is usually the most reliable.

Still, direct observation presents problems, and the reporter should not go about it in a haphazard way. Melvin Mencher, in his book *News Reporting and Writing*, points out that the reporter on assignment generally is confronted by a flood of facts: "A meeting can last two hours, cover seven different topics, and include four decisions. A speaker may deliver an address containing 4,500 words. To handle these stories, the reporter may have at most a column for each story, about 750 words."

Mencher suggests three major guidelines to selecting relevant facts:

1. *Know the community*: Develop a feeling and understanding of what readers need and want to know.

2. *Find the theme*: Carefully identify the theme of the story so that facts that support, buttress, and amplify the theme are collected.

3. *Look for the drama*: Develop a sensitivity to the unique, the "unusual, the break from the normal and routine."[1]

A reporter cannot be in two places at once and thus may miss an event. Or he may need further information about an event he observed. In such cases he turns to informed sources.

Cultivating news sources is a matter of energy, persistence, and attitude. The veteran reporter regularly contacts people with access to important information within the sphere of his coverage—whether the source is the Pentagon's information officer, a county clerk, a police desk sergeant, a switchboard operator at city hall, a scientist friend who explains complicated technical matters. The reporter develops a sense of friendship and mutual trust with the sources. In return for information, the reporter writes a fair account of the information provided him and protects the source from embarrassment and harm.

The smart reporter recognizes that information from a source may be vulnerable, because of the source's limited knowledge or vested interest. If there is any doubt, the reporter should corroborate the information from other sources, physical as well as human. There is a wide range of physical sources, from telephone books and newspaper clippings to records in government offices and reference books in libraries.

THE CHALLENGE OF ACCESS

All reporters, whether they are stationed at police headquarters or at the United Nations, face the challenge of gaining
access to information. The obstacles may be physical or the
reluctance of people to talk. Meeting the challenge can be
crucial to the reporter. Failure to obtain information quickly,
or to be at the right place at the right time, can mean the difference between completing a story by deadline or missing it.

When an airplane crashes on a rural hillside, for example,
the reporter must know how to reach the site quickly. He must
know which officials to consult for information about the crash.
He must find the most convenient and swiftest means of transmitting the information to his office.

When covering a complicated court proceeding, such as an
antitrust case, a reporter must know which dusty records will
yield the data he seeks, and which court officials are authorized
to explain procedural moves. When a reporter is investigating
a controversial government project, he must know how to wring
information out of officials who are reluctant to give it.

Although freedom of the press is generally taken for granted,
the First Amendment is not clear about open access to information. As a result, people who control the information that makes
news often make it difficult for reporters to get at the information. At the federal level, government officials withhold information for "security reasons." At state and county levels,
legislative committees sometimes hold secret meetings. At the
municipal level, officials may close their records to newsmen,
or police officers may refuse to divulge information about
arrests. By law, grand jury proceedings are not open to the press.

Private citizens may be even more reluctant to talk to reporters. There is no law that says a businessman or a doctor or
a clergyman must share information about an event with a
journalist. As Mitchell V. Charnley puts it in his book *Reporting*:

> The news sources may seek to remain silent for defensible reasons:
> That release of information would be damagingly premature, that it
> would invade privacy, or that they do not have authority to release
> it. They may also remain silent for causes the reporter rejects: em-
> barrassment about acts the reporter thinks the public has a right to
> know about, the wish to cover improper or even criminal behavior,
> or sometimes a misguided sense of "modesty."[2]

When a reporter is denied information he judges to be in the public interest, he must find other ways of digging out the facts. He can try another source, either human or physical, and another. If he has cultivated his sources well, he usually will come up with clues here and there, and can piece them together to make some sense. Often the original source, who at first refused to talk, will confirm information when confronted with clues obtained from second and third sources.

The challenge to broadcast journalists sometimes is greater than the challenge to print journalists. Some people tend to "clam up" when they know that their actions and words are being shown on television or recorded on tape. Cameras, still or television, generally are banned from the courtrooms on the ground that they are not consistent with fair and orderly procedure. Most legislative bodies at all levels of government frown on television coverage of their proceedings, although some extraordinary congressional hearings (for example, the Watergate investigations) have been televised.

In his book *The Rights of Reporters*, Joel M. Gora notes:

- The police cannot arbitrarily deny a press pass to a reporter.
- Except for reasonable restrictions on access to events behind police lines, the police cannot interfere with a reporter engaged in newsgathering activities in public places.
- Reporters cannot be denied access to open meetings of legislative or executive bodies.
- The reporter can try to use state law to open certain hearings of public bodies that have been closed as "executive sessions." But there is no Constitutional right to attend. Several states have adopted "sunshine laws" that require public agencies to open meetings and open records.
- Reporters do not have a Constitutional right to documents and records not available to the general public. (The Supreme Court has equated the press' right of access with the right of access to the public.) There are, however, state and federal laws granting access to official information.[3]

At the federal level, the Freedom of Information Act has facilitated access to the public records of executive branch bodies and independent regulatory agencies (the act does not apply to the legislative and judicial branches of the federal government). Requests for information usually involve search fees and reproduction costs and sometimes advance deposits. Nine categories of public records may be exempted from disclosure; these include information properly classified secret in the interest of national defense or foreign policy; privileged or confidential trade secrets or financial information; and certain investigatory records compiled for law-enforcement purposes. Some states have enacted similar statutes covering state records.

CHARACTERISTICS OF REPORTERS

To recognize the newsworthiness of an event, and to meet the challenges in gathering information about the event, the reporter must have certain personal qualities. Reporters tend to be independent and individualistic, but they nevertheless possess some common characteristics. Among them are the following:

Curiosity. The successful reporter wants to know everything about an event—not only the *what,* but also the *who, when, where, why,* and *how.* He is skeptical about information given him, and aggressively inquisitive in digging out detailed facts.

Creativity. To go beyond the obvious, the reporter must be creative and imaginative. He must think of alternative sources and be able to relate facts that may seem disparate. He must probe for both the causes and possible effects of an event.

Courage. It takes courage to go into dangerous places after a story, to question authority, to stray from the pack, to stand by convictions when they are doubted.

Endurance. Reporters often work long hours under difficult physical conditions. Covering a war is an obvious example, but a five-alarm fire or an airplane crash on an isolated mountain presents similar challenges, and persistence is required to get the necessary information.

Integrity. Commitment to the truth is the reporter's stock in trade. If he loses his credibility, his worth as a journalist is destroyed. He must be accurate down to the smallest detail.

Knowledgeability. To understand events and place them in proper perspective requires knowledge and awareness of what is going on in society. This quality enables the reporter to make best use of his curiosity and creativity, and to exploit his hunches and intuitions in pursuing a difficult story. To acquire such knowledge, the reporter must be willing to do research and plan in advance.

BASIC TOOLS

The journalist must master the use of certain tools of the trade if he or she hopes to perform efficiently and effectively.

The pencil and a note pad or wad of folded copy paper are the traditional tools of the reporter on assignment. The reporter should not rely on memory when obtaining information; he should take careful, legible notes that he can refer to later. If possible, the notes should be in some organized form to save time when they must be deciphered for writing the story on deadline. Since it is difficult to record words at conversational speed, knowledge of shorthand or speed writing is valuable. The wise reporter uses his travel time back to the office to unscramble his notes and organize his story before he starts to write.

The tape recorder is a necessity for the broadcast reporter, optional for the print reporter. It is useful for covering speeches and symposia and conducting long interviews. One drawback for the print reporter is that the tape must be transcribed. Another is the possibility of mechanical failure.

Despite the increasing automation of newsrooms, the typewriter still is a basic tool. Journalists should know how to type fast and accurately.

In automated newsrooms reporters work at computerized machines called video display terminals (VDT). They type on electronic keyboards and their typing is visible on a video screen above the keyboard. The machines produce electric impulses that go to a computer, and printouts can be made from the stored material. Although the new machines at first brought frowns to the brows of old-timers, the transition to electronics has proved to be quite painless for most journalists.

Facile use of the telephone is a "must" for every journalist. It saves time and jumps distance. It frequently gets behind closed doors. The phone is used continually for checking facts and calling in stories.

Every journalist regularly uses the dictionary and telephone book, and other references such as an almanac, a thesaurus, a style book, a grammar, and frequently *The Reader's Guide to Periodical Literature* and *The New York Times Index*.

GENERAL ASSIGNMENT

Most reporters on average newspapers are general-assignment newsgatherers. Unlike "beat" reporters, they do not go to the same places every day and check the same news sources. Rather, they roam the community as dictated by their daily assignments, which they usually do not know until they report to the city desk. They may cover a fire or a demonstration, a speech or a symposium, a death or a birth. Thus, they are generalists who must keep up with the events and issues of the community, and be capable of quick adjustments. New reporters are usually assigned to general reporting to "get their feet wet" on all kinds of stories.

Foreign correspondents are generalists of a different kind. They are experienced journalists who operate pretty much on their own far from the home office. Because they often are their newspapers' sole representatives in another country, they must cover every story that comes along, from a revolution to a diplomatic conference to an earthquake. National correspondents must meet the same demands, except that they cover large territories in the United States.

"BEATS"

"Beat" reporters are stationed in places where news happens regularly. These strategic locales include police and fire headquarters, city hall, the courts, the Board of Education. Much of the day's news comes from these sources. Most beat reporters go directly to their assigned posts in the morning and keep contact with their newsrooms by telephone. They are thoroughly familiar with the sources, procedures, and developing events on their beats, and can obtain information quickly. They are experienced at dictating a story on a sudden court verdict or a decision by the City Council.

Most Washington correspondents are beat reporters. The White House correspondent, for example, covers only the President and his entourage, and, along with the rest of the White House press corps, accompanies the Chief Executive when he travels. The Pentagon correspondent spends his time checking on news at the Defense Department. Correspondents who cover other federal departments and agencies follow a similar routine.

SPECIALISTS

Akin to the "beat" reporters are the specialists who have expertise in certain fields such as science, medicine, religion, education, law, business and finance, culture, labor, social behavior, sports. They have beats in the sense that they cover stories only in their field. They do not go to the same places every day, as the regular beat reporters do, but follow the specialized news as it develops. Many of their stories deal with trends rather than spot developments.

The purpose of the specialists is to provide, from their knowledge and experience, understanding and perspective to the trends in their complex fields. To maintain ability to do this, the specialists regularly read professional publications and consult with working professionals in their fields.

The specialist's role generally is a coveted goal on a newspaper, and is reached only after much experience either in journalism or in a specialized field.

INTERVIEWING

The interview is fundamental to all journalism. Whatever his assignment, the reporter must talk to people to obtain information. The more effective he is in conversation and asking questions, the better will be his information—and his story. There are two basic types of interviews.

One is the informal, impersonal interview to obtain information about an event or an issue. It can be quite simple. Checking a familiar source on the city hall "beat," for example, is a mini-interview. Or a reporter may arrive on the scene too late to observe a burglary, so he interviews an eyewitness or the store clerk or the police officer who responded to the alarm. In all likelihood he will interview all three, at least briefly. Except for identification and any circumstances pertinent to the burglary, the reporter is not interested in the interviewees personally, but in the information they can provide about the event.

The second type is the more formal personal interview, in

which the reporter is concerned with the individual and his or her views. This type, which results in an *interview story*, takes two forms: a *news interview* with an expert to elicit his or her views and comments on a subject of public interest; and a *personality interview*, with the purpose of writing a profile of the interviewee's life and character.

There are specific steps that should be followed for all interviews, but especially for the personal interview.

Before the Interview

1. Prepare in advance. This can be the key to success. Nothing can turn off an interviewee faster than a reporter who doesn't know what he's talking about. Research background information about the person, his work, the subjects likely to be discussed. Consult his friends to get anecdotes and others' views about the person. If the interviewee is an author, read his books; if he's a musician, listen to his recordings. Preparation enables the reporter to ask the right questions and understand the answers.

2. Settle on a theme so that the line of questioning will have purpose and logic. If possible, relate the theme to a current news development.

3. Work out a set of intelligent questions that will go beyond the obvious information obtained through research, and that will fulfill the theme.

4. Make an appointment at the interviewee's convenience in a place without distractions, such as an office or hotel room.

5. Be on time for the appointment, dressed appropriately, and prepared with all necessary materials.

6. Identify yourself immediately and state the purpose of the interview. Make clear that the material will be used and indicate how much time the interview is likely to take.

7. Clarify whether any of the interview will be off-the-record and not attributable to the source.

8. Ask the interviewee if he minds your using a tape recorder, if you have one, or taking notes while he talks.

During the Interview

1. From the outset, be a good listener. You're there to get specific information. Don't waste time by asking the obvious, by lecturing the source, arguing, or debating.

2. Tailor your overall approach to the interviewee. An aggressive attitude may suit a politician, but a casual mood may be more appropriate for an athlete or entertainer.

3. To put the interviewee at ease, start with easy questions. Then follow the set line of questioning in logical sequence, allowing one question to flow out of the previous one. Save the difficult questions until last. The reason is simple: The source may be angered by a difficult question and end the interview, but by that time you will have the other answers in hand.

4. If the source is reluctant to answer a question, skip it for the time being and try another approach later in the interview. By then he may feel more kindly toward the question. Suggest that a "no comment" will mean the story may be unbalanced or less accurate without his information.

5. If an answer suggests another line of questioning, deviate from the set questions, and then return later. But don't let the source stray off onto irrelevant tangents; the reporter should maintain control of the interview.

6. Don't be afraid of naïve or embarrassing questions. And if an answer is not exactly clear, ask for an explanation. Read back answers if requested or when in doubt about the phrasing of crucial material.

7. Observe the interviewee's dress and mannerisms, and confirm his vital statistics, such as name, address, age, education, jobs held, family.

8. Throughout the interview be accurate and thorough with your note-taking and get plenty of good quotes.

After the Interview

1. Review your notes. If you forgot an important question, or an answer is not entirely clear, check back with the source by telephone immediately.

2. Do further research that may be necessary for backgrounding points made by the interviewee.

DEPTH AND INVESTIGATIVE REPORTING

While all newsgathering involves some investigation, depth reporting and the probing process that has come to be known as "investigative reporting" have distinct attributes that set them apart from normal spot-news reporting. In recent years both depth and investigative reporting have become more prominent, especially in print journalism.

Depth reporting and investigative reporting are similar in that they go beyond the single news event, but they have a major difference: The depth reporter usually does not probe for *hidden* information (although he or she may), while the investigative reporter always does.

Depth Reporting. Depth reporting generally takes one of two forms:

1. It puts a single news event into a broad context, either by giving it historical perspective or by relating it to a current trend. An example might be the latest coup against a government, or an announcement of test scores indicating a continuing decline in students' reading ability.

2. Unlinked to any specific event, it explores a situation or issue of current public interest. An example might be the status of emergency care in the city's hospitals, or changing attitudes toward divorce.

Most newspapers and magazines, and many broadcast stations, now include depth reporting in their news operations. A widely admired model for this kind of reporting is the "leader" stories that appear on the front page of the *Wall Street Journal*. A "leader" dealing with the U.S. economy illustrates the nature of depth reporting. The story started as follows:

> Washington—The decline in the dollar's value abroad is putting President Carter in a trap from which there may be no good escape.
>
> Any action he can take, aides worry, risks economic and political troubles that might outweigh the hoped-for gains.
>
> Pressure is growing almost daily for Mr. Carter to strengthen the dollar by the main method at his disposal: forcing a cutback in the costly tide of U.S. oil imports that is blamed for much of the dollar's slide.
>
> Treasury Secretary Michael Blumenthal and Federal Reserve Board Chairman G. William Miller, almost abandoning hope of cutting imports through the delayed and weakened energy bill, are urging early presidential action; otherwise, they argue, the huge U.S. trade and international-payments deficits could swell further, the dollar grow weaker and U.S. inflation get worse because of rising prices of imports. By early May, unless the dollar strengthens, the pressure for presidential action could become almost irresistible.

The story then went on to cover these major elements:

1. The main weapons the President could use without congressional action—oil-import fees and import quotas—and their possible consequences.

2. Conflicting views of what caused the problem.

3. Effects of foreign fears about U.S. inflation.

4. Administration hopes for congressional action on the stalled energy bill.

5. Arguments for and against the key elements of the bill.

6. Different views of what is likely to happen if Congress does not pass the energy bill in the near future.[4]

Investigative Reporting. Although this type of reporting has been practiced since the muckraking period, it has intensified as government and society's institutions have grown bigger and more complex. Its primary purpose is the discovery of misbehavior, such as deceit and corruption, in public places. The classic example in the 1970s was the work of the *Washington Post*'s Robert Woodward and Carl Bernstein in ferreting out information about the Watergate scandal.

The distinguishing characteristic of investigative reporting is that the newsgatherer seeks information that information sources, for obvious reasons, prefer to keep secret. Prying out the information usually means persistent checking with scores of sources and painstaking exploration of written material. It takes all the curiosity, creativity, courage, endurance, and accuracy that a reporter can muster.

The process is described by Mitchell V. Charnley in *Reporting*:

> Investigative reporting differs from day-by-day leg work not in methods but rather in the circumstances that surround it—in the fact that the tip or idea on which it is based is more commonly obscure than sharply visible, that the reporting itself takes longer, demands more patience and perseverance and often imagination than everyday fact-gathering, that the reporter is likely to meet resistance, roadblocks, and often threats or genuine danger, and that the deadline may be not today's or tomorrow's, but that of a date months in the future.[5]

In their search for information about Watergate, Woodward and Bernstein spent months tracking down one source after another. The scandal started with a break-in at the Democratic National Committee offices in the Watergate building in Washington, and the two young reporters soon suspected that high officials in the Nixon administration were involved. They concentrated their search on the Committee to Re-Elect the President.

In an article about the Woodward-Bernstein work, James McCartney, national correspondent for the Knight newspapers, told how the reporters began ringing doorbells of committee members at night. McCartney said the reporters visited at least 50 homes, and he quoted Woodward:

> "It's like working on a murder story. You go to the people next door and ask them what they know about their neighbors, who the people were. If you call somebody at the White House on the telephone and ask for an appointment, they'll tell you no. But if you're standing out there on their front porch, facing them, they may let you in.
>
> "We'd ask questions. It would be a conversation they were in, or a book they had read, or a file that they saw. Sometimes people were downright unfriendly, but nevertheless helpful. It was like putting together a puzzle. You'd get a piece here, and a piece there, and you'd try to fit them together and see what kind of picture they made."[6]

Frequently the burden of investigation lies with physical, rather than human, sources. For their 1975 Pulitzer Prize–winning, seven-part investigative series about the Internal Revenue Service, "Auditing the I.R.S.," *Philadelphia Inquirer* reporters Donald L. Barlett and James B. Steele studied 20,000 tax lien notices, read 30,000 pages of records and transcripts, examined thousands more probate records, medical licensing records, mortgages, deeds, and records from regulatory agencies and the U.S. Senate.

The Barlett-Steele project illustrates how routine and tedious investigative reporting can be. To facilitate their fact-finding, Barlett and Steele and many other investigative reporters utilize computers and other sophisticated forms of data processing.

An example of how investigative reporters piece bits of information together into a whole was a 4,500-word story written by Seymour Hersh and published by the *New York Times*. The story was about a secret government project involving the sal-

vage of part of a Soviet submarine by a CIA ship. Contained in
the story was information gleaned from sources or documents of
the Ford administration, Congress, the CIA, the Navy, the
secretive Howard Hughes organization, a marine engineers'
union, and the crew of the salvage vessel. The story began as
follows:

> Washington, March 18—The Central Intelligence Agency financed
> the construction of a multimillion-dollar deep-sea salvage vessel and
> used it in an unsuccessful effort last summer to recover hydrogen-
> warhead missiles and codes from a sunken Soviet submarine in the
> Pacific Ocean, according to high Government officials.
>
> The salvage vessel, constructed under disguise for the C.I.A. by
> Howard R. Hughes, the reclusive billionaire industrialist, did suc-
> cessfully recover about one-third of the submarine, the officials said,
> but the portion raised from the ocean bottom did not include either
> the ship's missiles or its code room.
>
> Instead, the Government officials said, the C.I.A.-led expedition
> recovered the forward section of the ship containing the bodies of
> more than 70 Soviet seamen and officers who went down with the
> vessel when she mysteriously exploded in 1968 and sank in more
> than three miles of water.
>
> The Soviet submariners were buried at sea in military ceremonies
> that were filmed and recorded by C.I.A. technicians.
>
> Although thousands of scientists and workmen had security clear-
> ance for the program, known as Project Jennifer, the submarine
> salvage operation remained one of the Nixon and Ford Administra-
> tions' closest secrets.
>
> The Jennifer operation had provoked extended debate inside the
> United States intelligence community since the C.I.A. proposal to
> build the salvage vessel, with the cooperation of Mr. Hughes, first
> underwent high-level evaluation in the early 1970s.

The remainder of the story covered these main points:
1. Criticism and support of the project.
2. National security given as reason for secrecy.
3. Why Hughes was chosen to provide the cover.
4. Background of the salvage operation.
5. Dispute between the Navy and the CIA.
6. Facts about the Soviet submarine.
7. Facts about the salvage vessel, the *Glomar Explorer*.
8. Planning of the operation.

9. Objections to the plan.

10. Early clues in the press about the project.[7]

Small as well as large news organizations have investigative reporters, and investigations take place at the local and state levels as well as the national. As a guide for local news investigations, two veteran investigators, Clark Mollenhoff and John Siegenthaler, developed a "Check List for Investigative Reporters." The opening section, taken from a digest of the guide, indicates the scope of the information the investigative reporter might check in the form of "some common evils found in local government":

1. *Payroll Padding.* Check budget requests and payrolls to find whether they are loaded with relatives, friends, or political hacks. Who approves hiring? Are there deadheads or moonlighters on the payroll? How is a substantial increase in a payroll to be explained?

2. *Personnel: Hiring and qualifications.* Are there adequate civil service requirements and pension fund protections? Is the promotion system sound? Is there nepotism?

3. *Vacations, sick leave, work time.* Is supervision adequate? Could "dummy" employees be on the payroll, with higher-ups pocketing their pay?

4. *Property management and inventory control.* What special services (such as automobiles) are furnished to employees? How are they bought and paid for? Who gets the business and why? Where is control lodged? How does it work?

5. *False billing.* This practice is easy to conceal. A reporter can unearth it only by a direct check of all questionable items.

6. *Expenses*: Travel, per diem, etc. Are expense accounts padded? Is the mileage claimed and paid for actually traveled?

The guide then lists nine county or city offices to check for the information, suggesting specific processes and documents for exploration. For example, here is what is suggested for the Clerk of Court office:

Criminal indictments, grand jury reports. Are indictments properly disposed of? Are "old" reports or indictments being ignored?

Warrants handling. Are all warrants served? Are they properly issued? Are John Doe warrants used to conceal names of figures with "pull"?

Bail bonds. Is property offered for bonds properly assessed? Are professional bondsmen held rigidly to forfeitures? Are any bondsmen favored?

Witness fees. Are any such fees being collected improperly? If so, is there any kick-back to higherups? Are "dummy" witnesses being paid?

Jury selection. Are jury lists up to date? Is there danger of stacked panels? Do hand-picked jurymen get selected—a strong union man, for instance, on a labor case?

Civil suits. Look for conflict of interest. Watch for financial details of damage suits.[8]

LEGAL RESTRAINTS

Although the First Amendment protects the press from governmental interference, the press does not have complete freedom. There are laws against libel and invasion of privacy, and certain limitations on newsgathering.

Libel. Libel is any false and malicious writing or picture that holds up a person to public ridicule, hatred, or contempt, or causes injury to his reputation. Published material likely would be judged defamatory if it tended to injure a person in his occupation; implied commission of a crime, lack of chastity, mental incapacity, or a loathsome disease; or damaged a person's credit. Such material, in most cases, would be safe for publication if it is privileged—that is, from a public and official proceeding—and is true and without malice.

Since 1964 the Supreme Court has relaxed the libel restraints in cases involving public officials and public figures. Such persons cannot recover damages for defamation unless they can prove the material false and published with "active malice."

Privacy. The right of privacy is designed to protect a person's peace of mind, feelings, and sensibilities. Invasion of privacy is said to occur when an individual is exposed to publicity and suffers mental distress as a consequence. Journalists cannot intrude upon people's private domains to seek out news and make public what is private.

Limitations on Newsgathering. In his book *News Reporting and Writing*, Melvin Mencher summarizes the limitations succinctly:

The press has no right to attend grand jury proceedings, conferences of the Supreme Court, executive sessions of official bodies and the meetings of private organizations. Although censorship is prohibited, courts have ordered the press not to publish what the courts consider prejudicial information about a criminal trial, and books have been examined to eliminate what the courts have ruled to be information vital to national security.

The Supreme Court has not decided whether a reporter can be punished for what he publishes, but reporters have been jailed for contempt for refusing to identify sources and for publishing grand jury proceedings. Shield laws in some states protect a reporter from having to reveal his sources, but in others he may be jailed for contempt if he does not.[9]

NOTES

1. Melvin Mencher, *News Reporting and Writing* (Dubuque, Iowa: Wm. C. Brown Company Publishers, 1977), p. 28.
2. Mitchell V. Charnley, *Reporting* (New York: Holt, Rinehart and Winston, Inc., 1966), p. 97.
3. Joel M. Gora, *The Rights of Reporters* (New York: Avon Books, 1974), pp. 73–96.
4. *Wall Street Journal*, April 3, 1978, p. 1.
5. Charnley, p. 279.
6. James McCartney, "The *Washington Post* and Watergate: How Two Davids Slew Goliath," *Columbia Journalism Review*, July–Aug. 1973, pp. 14–15.
7. *New York Times*, March 19, 1975, p. 1.
8. Charnley, pp. 280–282.
9. Mencher, p. 279.

SUGGESTED READING

Charnley, Mitchell V. *Reporting*. New York: Holt, Rinehart and Winston, Inc., 1966.

Mencher, Melvin. *News Reporting and Writing*. Dubuque, Iowa: Wm. C. Brown Company Publishers, 1977.

Strentz, Herbert. *News Reporting and News Sources*. Ames, Iowa: Iowa State University Press, 1978.

Warren, Carl. *Modern News Reporting*. New York: Harper & Row, 1959.

10
How the News Is Written and Edited

Good news writing for both print and broadcasting has two basic qualities: (1) It is informative, providing adequate facts so that the reader or listener learns and understands exactly what has happened; and (2) it is interesting, using journalistic techniques and patterns that encourage the reader or listener to follow a story to the end. News writing demands intelligence, discipline, and hard work; but it also requires perception, sensitivity, imagination, creativity, good taste, and wit.

Once the reporting has been completed, news writing starts with advance thinking and planning to achieve proper focus on the theme and logical development of the story. Selection and composition of the lead is crucial, because the lead establishes the tone of the story and sets up the organization of the story units. While all news writing generally conforms to traditional formats and ground rules, there are differences between spot-news stories and feature, magazine, and broadcast stories.

Editing and headlines, which require special skills on the part of the journalist, are essential complements to news writing. Editing sharpens and polishes the writing to make it as informative and interesting as possible. Headlines attract attention to the writing and summarize what can be learned from it.

ADVANCE PLANNING

A reporter returning to his newsroom after covering a story usually is faced with two facts of journalistic life. First, he has a scramble of notes and thoughts from his observations, interviews, and research. Second, he has finite limits on the time and space in which to write his story: that is, he must meet a specific deadline for completion of his writing, and he must confine his story to the length determined by his editors. To reconcile these conditions, the writer must organize his information. He must think before he writes. He must sift through his material and work out a plan that will lead to a clear and cohesive story within the time and space allotted him.

Many noted writers and teachers have stressed the need for a plan. In *The Elements of Style*, the "little book" familiar to generations of college English students, William Strunk, Jr., and E. B. White offer typical advice: "Choose a suitable design and hold to it. A basic structural design underlies every kind of writing. . . . The first principle of composition, therefore, is to foresee or determine the shape of what is to come and pursue that shape."[1]

The advance thinking should address questions such as these: What do I want to say? What is the basic idea, or theme, of the story? What is the nature of my audience—average readers or experts in the field I am writing about? What questions would the audience want answered? What points in my notes are irrelevant to the theme and should be discarded? How much supporting and explanatory material is necessary to make the theme understandable to my audience? Which quotes, anecdotes, and examples would add interest and advance the story development?

The answers to these questions suggest the plan or design of the story. The plan should conform to the basic organization of a straight news story: a beginning (the lead), a middle (the body, or development), and an end (the conclusion, which is optional and found most often in feature stories).

From his notes, the reporter selects the main point that will provide the theme focus of his lead. Then he organizes the material to fit into the basic structure that applies to most news stories: (a) explanation or amplification of the lead; (b) any necessary background; (c) secondary or less important information. Only when the reporter completes this procedure, and sees clearly where his story is headed, should he begin to write.

WRITING TIPS

No two news stories are exactly alike in shape and content, and each story reflects the individual writing style of its author. Nevertheless, well-written stories have common characteristics that make them "readable," understandable, and meaningful.

Information. A news story should be as complete with facts as possible. There should be no "gaps" in the account that leave questions unanswered and the reader guessing. At the minimum, the story should cover the five W's and H: *What* happened and *who* was involved? *Where* and *when* did it happen? *Why* did it happen and *how*?

Most news stories nowadays also include background and explanatory material that place the immediate event into a broad context and suggest its significance. This material answers the question, "So what?" For example, if a story relates the development of a new vaccine, it should compare the new vaccine with existing ones. If a church denomination changes its position on women in the clergy, the news story should explain the trends in other denominations.

Human Interest. It is an axiom in news writing that people are more interested in other people than in abstract ideas, policies, decisions. This accounts for the attention given to births and deaths, engagements and marriages, accidents and arrests. Stories about children are sure winners.

Thus, the reporter should try to personalize the news by translating it into human terms. A story about a cutback in a community's welfare budget comes to life if the reporter tells it from the viewpoint of a welfare family.

The technique is to find a representative person who is affected or involved in the news development, and write about him or her as an example of the situation or its causes or consequences.

Selectivity. One of the hardest things for a journalist to learn is selectivity: knowing what to include in a story and what to leave out. This requires intuitive editorial judgment that comes with experience.

Reporters hate to discard information that took time and sweat to gather, even though it may be irrelevant to the theme. Or they may not be sure whether certain information is pertinent, so they stick it in and pass the decision to the editor. The result is a story that is overlong and bogs down with unnecessary material.

On the other hand, brevity is not always possible. Some stories are so complex that they require an extended account with scene-setting and background; they would be incomplete without it. In exercising selectivity, the writer should gauge his audience in terms of the well-known rule of thumb in newsrooms: "Never underestimate your reader's intelligence, but don't overestimate his facts."

The trick is to relate the available material to the story design. The reporter runs through his notes and decides whether each point is or is not relevant to the story development he has in mind.

Clarity. News writing serves its purpose only if people read it or listen to it, and studies have shown that people prefer stories that are easy to understand. Here are some suggestions for making news writing clear:

• A good starting point is a broad admonition from Strunk and White: Be specific, not general; be definite, not vague; be concrete, not abstract. The authors provide an example: "A period of unfavorable weather set in" is less effective than "It rained every day for a week."[2]

• Use simple rather than fancy words. News writing should avoid "averred" when "said" will do the job. "Many" is better than "multitudinous." Most editors advise, "Write as you talk."

• Clichés, jargon, and gobbledygook are a sign of lazy writing and are excised by most copy editors. Clichés are tired and worn words and phrases that are so familiar that they make most readers groan. Jargon is specialized language common to a specialized field, and usually unfamiliar to a majority of readers. Gobbledygook is the foggy and pretentious prose used widely in documents of the government, military, legal affairs, and other institutions. Some examples:

rendezvous with destiny (cliché).
let the chips fall where they may (cliché).

busy as a bee (cliché).
blast-off (space jargon).
grilled (police jargon).
crisis (journalism jargon).
like-minded percentagewise (gobbledygook).
One cannot ad hoc tax reform (gobbledygook, from a U.S. Treasury official).

Clichés should be shunned at all times. Jargon and gobbledygook sometimes cannot be avoided; in such cases they should be explained in layman's terms.

• Nouns and verbs should be emphasized; adjectives and adverbs should be used sparingly. Specific nouns and verbs provide force, vigor, and color. Although adjectives and adverbs are indispensable parts of speech, they should not be used as substitutes for nouns and verbs in conveying meaning. A useful writing rule is "show, don't tell." Rather than saying that something is "unusual," let the nouns and verbs "show" the situation so that the reader says, "That's unusual."

• A widely accepted principle is one idea to a sentence. There are exceptions, but the principle is regarded as a means of keeping news writing simple and direct. Similarly, to avoid confusion, a new paragraph should be started when there is a change of subject or speaker. With both sentences and paragraphs, short is better than long.

Conciseness. "Keep it tight" and "don't waste words" are familiar orders around a newsroom. They mean: eliminate all unnecessary words, redundancies, and repetitions. There are two reasons for the order: First, concise writing is vigorous and to the point, and thus more easily understood than rambling writing. Second, tight writing occupies less space than loose writing, which means more stories can be squeezed into a newspaper or newscast. Strunk and White point out that "this requires not that the writer make all his sentences short, or that he avoid all detail and treat his subjects only in outline, but that every word tell."[3]

Some examples:

Unnecessary words. "He is a man who" can be simply "he." "The problem is a difficult one" can be shortened to "The problem is difficult." "Now" is better than "at the present time."

Redundancies. In "true facts" the "true" can be dropped because facts are always true. With "consensus of opinion," the "of opinion" is unnecessary because consensus means opinion.

Active Voice. The active is usually more direct, concise, and forceful than the passive. "He tossed the bag of tools over the fence" is preferable to "The bag of tools was tossed over the fence by him." Whenever possible, the sentence should have the simple, direct construction: subject-verb-object.

Pace. One of the most neglected, but important, aspects of writing is pace—the rate at which the writing presents information. Writing should be paced so that the reader will be able to understand what he or she is reading, without having to stop or reread. Pace is especially important when the writing deals with complex, technical material.

In his book *Communicating Technical Information,* Robert R. Rathbone explains that the pace is too rapid if the reader's mind lags behind his eye; and the pace is too slow if the reader's mind wanders ahead of his eye (or wants to).[4]

The news writer must be conscious of pace because daily news reports are full of complicated developments in politics and government, business and finance, science and medicine that must be written in a way that the average reader can understand them.

Tone. Tone refers to the quality and attitude reflected in the writing: serious, frivolous, high-class, low-class, youthful, sophisticated. Tone should be consistent. If the story is about a serious subject, the writer should not inject levity.

SOME GROUND RULES

All news writing follows certain ground rules related to both content and style. The rules are designed to promote uniformity and fairness in the presentation of news.

Accuracy. Credibility is absolutely essential to a reporter if he is to be effective in his job. Therefore he must be accurate with both his facts and his word usage. He must verify information such as names and figures given by sources.

Attribution. Every news story should have a source whenever it is clear that information does not come from the reporter's direct observation. The story should indicate the origin of the information and the relative worth of the source. Attribution is not necessary in references to matters of accepted, common knowledge. According to John Hohenberg in *The Professional Journalist*:

> The best attribution is to name the source. The next best is the name of the organization, office, or group represented by the source as spokesman. The least satisfactory, but sometimes the most necessary, is some variation of the phrase, "informed source," if the origin of news must be held in confidence. Only columnists, commentators, and similarly privileged characters are entitled to use themselves as the authority for the correctness of their news, and withhold all mention of sources. Such a privilege does not extend to the ordinary news writer.[5]

Fairness. The press is the surrogate voice of all the people. Therefore, traditionally news writing has been characterized by balance and fairness. Both sides of a controversy and all viewpoints on an issue generally are presented. If a politician makes an accusation against his opponent, fairness requires that a reporter seek out the target and get his reply.

Balance and fairness are related to objectivity. Historically news writing has stressed objectivity, that is, it has been based on observable facts and has been free of the reporter's opinion. As Melvin Mencher notes in *News Reporting and Writing*: "News is objective when it can be checked against some kind of record—the text of a speech, the minutes of a meeting, a police report, a purchase voucher, a payroll, unemployment data or vital statistics. The reporting of facts that can be measured and verified is the mainstay of journalism in the United States."[6]

But as Mencher also points out, objectivity can be limiting; it encourages passivity. It does not take into account that what somebody says may not be true. It leaves the monitoring of events and statements, and judgments of the possible consequences, to the bureaucracy or special-interest groups. Thus, objective journalism sometimes falls short of providing the public with thorough and balanced information on which to base decisions. For this reason, since the 1950s news writing has increasingly included interpretation along with the objective reporting of facts.

There are those who feel that news writing and presentation can never be truly objective. They point out that the reporter makes a subjective judgment when he decides which facts to include in his story and which to leave out. Editors make a subjective judgment when they decide to emphasize a story by putting it on the front page, or deemphasize it by putting it on a back page.

Nevertheless, as Mencher notes, "Objectivity is still the reporter's basic state of mind as he or she approaches a story."[7] Bound by the professional standards of journalism, and monitored by the public and his competition, the responsible news writer aims at fairness and balance.

Good Taste. Responsible news writing avoids material that unnecessarily harms or embarrasses persons in the news. Such material includes sexual matters, physical handicaps, extreme violence, and obscenity.

Past Tense. Traditionally straight news has been written in the past tense on the ground that the event being reported has already happened. Interpretive and trend stories, however, often are written in the present tense because the events or issues being covered are continuing.

Third Person. Straight news generally is written impersonally in the third person. The second-person "you" construction, which addresses the reader directly, is considered weak. The first-person "I" or "we" construction, which injects the writer into the story, is used only on rare occasions when the recounting of personal experiences is specially suitable.

Written Form. Because of the large quantity of news stories, and the need for speed in the processing of the stories, there is a common, convenient form for preparation of copy. The major elements:

1. For identification, the reporter's name and story slug (an identifying label) are written in the upper left-hand corner of all pages.

2. The writing on the first page starts about halfway down the page to allow room at the top for a headline or editor's instructions.

3. Stories are typed double-spaced to allow room between the lines for editing alterations and symbols.

4. Each page should end with the end of a paragraph, so that

each page can be handled individually as deadline approaches.

5. Each page is numbered consecutively. Except for page one, each page has only a small margin at the top. Margins on the sides are at least one inch wide.

6. To indicate the end of the story, the writer types the old telegrapher's symbol "30" after the last line of copy.

7. All news writing follows the news organization's mechanical rules of style for capitalization, abbreviation, spelling, and grammar. Most news organizations use the stylebooks of the Associated Press and United Press International, but some have their own.

In newsrooms that have been automated, the form and procedure for preparing copy have been changed somewhat because computerized terminals have replaced typewriters. The basic rules, however, still apply.

THE LEAD

The lead, or beginning, is the most important part of a news story, both in newspapers and in broadcast news. It is the "come-on." What the lead says almost always determines whether the reader or listener will continue with the story or skip to something else. If the lead fails to grab the attention and curiosity of the reader or listener, the rest of the story could be wasted. The news writer, therefore, struggles with the lead. He devotes a major share of his time and effort to both the content and the form.

Although there are several types of leads, all should accomplish two functions: They should "grab" the reader and entice him to read on; and they should set out the story theme so that the reader has a clue to what he is going to read about. The lead should be direct, compact, to the point, sharply honed, dramatic.

Some Classics. Whenever journalists talk about sharp leads, the following usually are recalled as among the most memorable:

Snow, followed by small boys on sleds.
—H. Allen Smith, *New York World-Telegram*, a weather forecast.

The million-to-one shot came in. Hell froze over. A month of Sundays hit the calendar. Don Larsen today pitched a no-hit, no-run, no-man-reach-first game in a World Series.

—Shirley Povich, *Washington Post & Times Herald,* on the perfect game the Yankee pitched against the Brooklyn Dodgers in 1956.

The state of New Jersey, which spent $1.2 million to capture and convict Bruno Richard Hauptmann, executed him tonight with a penny's worth of electricity.

Before his body ever hung loose and heavy against the straps of the electric chair, officials collected from witnesses a dozen affidavits, swearing that Hauptmann had died in the place, time, and manner prescribed by law. Then they closed their four-year file on the murder of Charles A. Lindbergh, Jr.

—Harry Ferguson, UPI editor.

The Past. There was a time, starting a century ago, when the lead was regarded as a one-sentence summary of the entire story. The sentence was crammed with facts about the *what, who, when, where, why*—and perhaps the *how.* This kind of lead, made prominent by the press associations, traces back to the invention of the telegraph, which facilitated reporting from a distance and put a new emphasis on being "first with the news." Eager to get their "scoops," at least the gists of them, into print, correspondents in the field telegraphed summaries that were rushed into type as leads. They followed with the most important details, and then the secondary material. Often the leads were so long and crowded that they were a burden to read and a challenge to comprehend.

The Present. Later, as radio emerged as a competitor and communications and printing technology improved, the newspaper imperative to be first in a tight space eased, and so did the imperative for all of the five W's and H in a one-sentence summary. It was all right for a lead to consist of two or three sentences, or even two or three paragraphs if the story was long and complex. Some of the W's could be dropped to the second or third paragraph. The lead might not be a directly stated summary at all, but an indirect, or delayed, approach with an anecdote, a quotation, or a question. The reason for the changes was to make leads more interesting—and therefore enticing—and more comprehensible. That kind of thinking governs leads today.

In the urge to be clever and interesting, however, the news writer must not forget that the fundamental reason for the lead is to tell the news. The opening should make clear the theme around which the story is unified. Although the five-W's-and-H formula no longer monopolizes the lead, it still is the constant on which the lead and body of the story are based.

The Approach. All leads fall into the two broad categories of *direct* and *delayed* (or *indirect*). The direct lead, which is used on most "hard" news stories, states in straightforward fashion the central facts of what happened. The delayed lead, which is used most frequently on features or "soft" news, "backs into" the story with an anecdote or description or quotation that establishes a mood or a scene. A good delayed lead also includes a word or a phrase that signals the story theme.

It is not uncommon for a writer to spend as much time on the lead as on the rest of the story. The reason is that the lead is pivotal; it sets the tone and direction for the whole story.

The key to success is advance thinking. In reviewing and analyzing his material, the writer seeks answers to these questions: *What* was the most significant development, or change, in the event covered? *Who* was involved, through action or words? The answers constitute the basic news. The next step is to devise the most interesting form in which to present the answers. Melvin Mencher suggests three parts to this step:

1. Is a direct or a delayed lead best?
2. Is there a colorful word or dramatic phrase I want to work into the lead?
3. What is the subject, and what verb best will move the reader into the story?[8]

Basic Guidelines. Modern journalism allows the news writer considerable latitude with leads, but some traditional guidelines still apply to most straight-news stories. Among them are:

1. Keep it short and compact. A lead should not extend beyond 30 words, except in unusual cases, and if possible should be held to under 25 words.

2. Open with a sharp, direct statement of the key fact that tells the reader what the story is about. An old newsroom axiom says that the theme should be evident by the sixth word of the opening sentence.

3. Use the subject-verb-object construction for clarity. Avoid opening with a prepositional phrase ("At a meeting of the Lions

Club last night . . .") or a participial phrase ("Meeting at the YMCA, the Lions Club . . .").

4. Keep the lead simple and uncluttered. An opening confined to one incident or idea is likely to be more readily understood—and therefore more effective—than one with several.

5. Try for clear, punchy words that typify the content and tone of the story. Be precise, not general. A rule-of-thumb test for a good lead is: Does it immediately suggest a headline to the copy editor? If it does not, the theme is not clearly defined.

6. Emphasize people rather than things and abstract concepts.

7. Avoid "calendar" leads that merely "list" an event without specifically reporting what happened or what was said. For example:

Kill this "calendar" lead:

> James Barber, deputy commissioner of the Health Department, spoke to the Rotary Club last night about pollution of the Hudson River.

The reason for the kill? The lead does not report anything that Barber said. It creates an expectation that is not satisfied. An intelligent reader immediately thinks, "Yes, yes, but what did he *say*?"

8. Emphasize the attribution if the source of information is especially important; deemphasize it if the source is not especially important. Use the name if it is well known. Some editors prefer the attribution at the beginning of the sentence; others prefer it at the end. Following is an example in which the name of the source is important and therefore is stressed:

> Secretary of State Henry Kissinger announced today that he would re-open nuclear arms talks with the Soviet Union next week.

The attribution should be as unobtrusive and condensed as possible. In most cases the name can be held until the second paragraph and a long official title can be replaced by a succinct characterizing phrase. The expertise of a source should be emphasized. A revision of the Rotary Club example above illustrates these techniques:

> A pollution specialist said last night that a health hazard has been created by the discharge of toxic wastes by chemical companies into the Hudson River.

The expert, James Barber, deputy commissioner of the New York State Department of Health, pointed out that nine communities use the polluted Hudson as a source of their drinking water. Barber spoke at a meeting of the Rotary Club.

Direct Leads. Direct leads hit the news immediately. They deal with one or more of the five W's and H, and they are used on the majority of stories. There are several forms of the direct lead, but the most common is the summary.

Here is a breakdown of a *summary* lead incorporating the five-W formula:

Who?—John Chambers, a bricklayer, 16 Drake Road.
What?—broke his leg.
When?—today.
Where?—construction site on the waterfront.
Why?—scaffolding collapsed and he fell.

John Chambers, a bricklayer of 16 Drake Rd., broke his leg today when scaffolding collapsed and he fell at a construction site on the waterfront.

Which W gets the emphasis depends on the nature of the story and the commonsense judgment of the writer. The example above stresses the *who*. Another kind of *who* lead would be one involving a prominent person: "Senator Edward Kennedy toured the nuclear power plant today. . . ." The important point is not the tour, but the fact that a well-known Senator made the tour; the story would not be newsworthy if unknown John Smith made the tour.

The following is an example of a simple, straightforward *what* lead. The story on which it appeared was one of a series on police corruption that earned the *Indianapolis Star* the 1975 Pulitzer Prize for special local reporting.

A Criminal Court jury last night convicted Mary Martin, Northside brothel operator, of prostitution and recommended she be sentenced to a term of 2 to 5 years in prison.

In this story the conviction is the news and therefore is stressed in the lead.

A more involved *what* lead, one based on a long investigation rather than a specific timely event such as the jury action above, is illustrated by the following lead on the first installment of the *Indianapolis Star* series:

> Widespread corruption in the Indianapolis Police Department—including graft and protection for prostitution, narcotics, bootlegging, and gambling—has been uncovered in a six-month investigation by the *Indianapolis Star*.
>
> Involvement in corruption by dozens of Indianapolis policemen is not limited to taking money, but has led some members of the department into criminal activities, the probe showed.

Where becomes the focus of a lead if an important or unusual place is involved and is key to the story:

> The White House was the target today of farmers picketing in protest against the President's agriculture policies.

When is the significant element in a situation like this.

> Just as the judge was about to send the manslaughter case of Mary Brown to the jury, one of the defense lawyers dashed into the courtroom and announced that he had discovered new evidence.

Delayed Leads. This kind of lead does not get to the news directly and immediately, but establishes a scene or mood with a description, anecdote, or quotation. It is used most often on soft news and features, but also is appropriate for hard news on occasion.

Thomas Fitzpatrick of the *Chicago Sun-Times* won a Pulitzer Prize for a story he wrote in 1969 about a demonstration by the Weathermen faction of the Students for a Democratic Society, which erupted into confrontations with police. Fitzpatrick started as follows:

> Bad Marion had been standing in front of the fire he had made of the Lincoln Park bench for 30 minutes, shouting to everyone in the crowd and warning them how bad he was.
>
> It was 10:25 p.m. and I kept looking to the north where the police had set up their command post in the Lincoln Park Cultural Arts Center.

Deputy Chief Robert Lynskey had told me he'd be coming to the park at 10:30 to see how the situation was developing.

"Maybe we won't even have to tell them to leave," he said about two hours earlier. "Maybe by that time they'd all be tired and want to go on their own."

But they weren't tired, and now about 200 of the kids began racing out of the park, heading toward the Chicago Historical Society. Bad Marion started running too, brandishing a long piece of burning board in his right hand.

A good quote usually attracts the reader's attention, and often can sum up a situation more interestingly than a direct lead can. Quote leads should be used only when the quote is especially apt or colorful, or when it is well known and fits the situation perfectly. The following lead, for example, is appropriate because it establishes a mood, introduces conflict and suspense, and tells the reader the results of a meeting the night before:

"It looks like the buses will stop running. Unless something I don't know about suddenly comes out of the blue, we're sure to have a strike—and it could be a long one."

James Burns, chief negotiator for the bus drivers' union, puffed on a cigarette as he spoke to newsmen this morning in the corridor of City Hall. He appeared weary after a night of contract talks with transportation department officials.

Both Burns and Charles Perkins, the city's chief negotiator, said last night's meeting failed to break the deadlock over the city's proposal to reduce the number of bus drivers. The meeting was the 15th since the drivers' contract expired on March 1.

Even with a delayed lead, it is important that the theme of the story is clear right away. This can be accomplished with a word or phrase that provides a clue. In the lead above the key word is "buses"—which signals the subject—and the rest of the phrase tells the reader that last night's meeting failed to break the deadlock.

STORY DEVELOPMENT

Once the writer decides on the theme and composes the lead around the theme, he or she must organize the rest of the material to produce a coherent story that flows logically out of the lead. The purpose of the body of the story is to elaborate on and explain the news summarized in the lead. The story may or may not have a formal conclusion, depending on the pattern chosen for developing the story.

There are three basic forms for organizing the news story: inverted pyramid, chronological account, and suspended interest with conclusion.

Inverted Pyramid. This term refers to the shape of the story as defined by the importance of the facts used. It simply means that the story, like an inverted pyramid, is top-heavy: the most important material is put at the beginning, and the least important is put at the end. This is the classic pattern for straight-news stories, and it is the norm for stories that start with a summary lead.

There are two reasons for the popularity of the inverted pyramid. First, it meets the needs of busy media users. Most people want to know what happened right away; and if they are stirred by the essential facts at the beginning of the story, they will continue to the details. Second, the inverted pyramid is convenient for journalists, who must conform to the physical limitations of their business; if they run out of time and space for a story, they can easily trim the least important material from the bottom without harming the fundamental elements of the story.

The inverted pyramid form is used for most news stories, although its use has declined with the trend toward more interpretive and feature stories. The inverted pyramid is the standard for the wire services, which edit and trim their stories continually at relay points to meet the varying needs of their diversified clients.

Despite the virtues of the inverted pyramid form, some communicators feel that it is a wasteful anachronism that has been overtaken by electronic journalism. They argue that the pattern forces repetition in presentation of the news: the headline, the summary lead, the body that elaborates on the lead. And they contend that there is no need for newspapers to summarize news that has already been presented in capsule form by the broadcast media.

Writing news in inverted pyramid form requires advance thought and careful planning. Because this kind of story is not told in the sequential order that it happened, the writer must pay close attention to coherence. The story must be built unit by unit, in descending order of importance. Relationships between events and ideas must be clear. Transitions must be smooth.

Related material should be kept together; each theme should be completed, at least with the essential facts, before moving on to the next theme. There should be no jumping back and forth. The exception to this procedure is the complex event that may be made clearer if there is a second, more detailed elaboration of certain points. In such a case, near the end of the story the writer may jump back to a theme already treated in general terms.

In sum, most news stories fit into a simple structure as follows:

1. The lead, which establishes the theme and summarizes the event.

2. The material that explains and amplifies the lead.

3. The background necessary to put the event into a broad context or trend and give it meaning.

4. The secondary or less important material.

Chronological Account. This is a convenient way to handle a complex story or one involving action or a series of related events. This form is used commonly for accident and law-enforcement stories. Once the lead sets out the theme, and one or two paragraphs capsulize the overall story, the narrative picks up the event at the beginning and describes what happened in chronological order.

A chronological account usually has a conclusion: the final episode in the sequence of events, or a statement of fact, outside the chronology, that provides an end or rounds out the story. In either case, the ending cannot be chopped off indiscriminately as with an inverted-pyramid story.

Suspended-Interest. Sometimes called the pyramid form because it withholds the most important point until last, the suspended-interest development is used mainly for short, catchy "brighteners," but occasionally for longer features. This form does not have a summary at the beginning, and the story generally is developed chronologically. It cannot be trimmed at the end.

Because the suspended-interest story works up to the climax near the end (a reversal of the inverted pyramid), this form is attractive to journalists who believe there should be more storytelling qualities in journalism. In a "brightener," the climax may be a punch line; in a feature, the climax may be the most revealing or informative or interesting episode.

FEATURE STORY

A feature story has been described broadly as "anything that is not a news story." More specifically, Daniel R. Williamson, in his book *Feature Writing for Newspapers*, offers this definition: "A feature story is a creative, sometimes subjective, article designed primarily to entertain and to inform readers of an event, a situation, or an aspect of life."[9]

Always a staple of journalism, the feature now is used extensively in both the print and the broadcast media. It provides a change of pace from the largely negative tendency of most hard news; at the same time, it is a convenient mechanism for exploring the complex conditions of modern living. In recent years the feature has become increasingly prominent in the print media as the immediacy of broadcast reporting has forced newspapers and magazines to deemphasize speed and seek alternative treatments of the news.

A feature story usually is not perishable; that is, unlike a straight-news story, which loses its interest once the event has been reported, the feature is not pegged to a specific time element. Most features remain usable for days, weeks, even months.

The basic writing techniques that apply to straight-news stories apply also to feature stories. However, writing features affords more freedom and flexibility in the choice and treatment of a subject. For this reason, most journalists try to write features, either as a full-time assignment or as an adjunct to their general or "beat" reporting.

Types. Within the broad definition, there are two categories of feature stories.

1. The *news feature*, or *"sidebar,"* is a spin-off from, or supplement to, a hard-news story. The purpose of a sidebar is not to entertain, but to inform, to humanize the news, to illuminate the significance of an event through in-depth reporting and writing. A sidebar accompanies a hard-news story and provides background and/or interpretation of the event reported in the main story, or detailed elaboration of a key point for which there is no room in the main story. A sidebar could be a personality profile, a historical perspective, a roundup of reaction to an event, a description of a mood or an environment. The sidebar approach is discussed more fully in the next chapter.

2. The *"human-interest" story* is intended to entertain and to spotlight the nature and living habits of people. This classic type usually has no specific time element, although it generally is placed in a current or seasonal context. It rarely has news value in the sense that a hard-news story does; rather it caters to people's curiosity about other people, about animals, about oddities, about unusual things and places. The key to human-interest features is not significance but emotional response— whether it be laughing or crying, sympathy or anger.

Most human-interest angles are familiar; only the characters and circumstances change from year to year. Here are some tried-and-true feature situations:

• Children: A young Vietnamese refugee is adopted by an American family; an eleven-year-old chess player holds his own against a recognized adult master.

• Animals: A lost dog turns up two months later; elephants from the circus parade on Main Street.

• Oddity: the birth of sextuplets; the patriot who paints his house red, white, and blue.

• Drama: A mountain climber scales the exterior of the World Trade Center; a police officer persuades a distraught man not to jump off the roof.

• Humor: The Internal Revenue Service official who is called in for an audit of his tax return; a flag is inadvertently flown upside down in front of City Hall.

• Pathos: An elderly couple is evicted with no place to go; a contractor bulldozes a huge hole in the wrong backyard.

• Seasonal: A family has no Christmas presents for the children; a singing telegram service specializes in Valentine greetings.

• Color (mood or scene): Loyal fans wait in line 15 hours for the first tickets to the basketball playoffs; owners pick through their stores after a night of looting during a blackout.

Writing Techniques. Feature writing offers the writer an opportunity to use his creativity and imagination. The potential for human interest is everywhere. And rarely is there deadline pressure for completing a story; because most features are exclusive, the writer does not have to worry about competition and he normally has plenty of time for research, reporting, and quality writing.

The principles that apply to straight-news writing also apply to features. There should be advance planning of the theme, the material to be gathered, the selection of relevant material to be included, the organization of the material into a focused and coherent story. The writing should be clear, concise, compact. Sentences should be direct and, for the most part, short. There is, however, room for more descriptive and stylish flourishes than are found in hard-news writing. Basically, the feature writer is a storyteller who tries to draw the reader or listener into the situation he is relating.

LEAD. Since a feature is not based on developing news, a summary at the beginning is not vital. More often than not, a feature can start with a delayed lead. If a summary is used, it should be brief, and composed so as to stimulate curiosity and involvement of the reader or listener in the story.

DEVELOPMENT. The inverted pyramid form can be used, but, unlike a straight-news story, the feature usually has an ending that should not be cut off. Both the chronological account and the surprise-ending forms are popular in features because they are natural for storytelling. Paragraphs should be short, and each should elaborate on an item from the preceding paragraph to keep the story moving.

ENDING. The ending depends on the type of feature. A story told in chronological order usually builds up to a climax—a logical outcome of a sequence of events. A summary ending draws a conclusion from the body of the story, and generally refers back to the theme established in the lead. An oddity story or brightener usually has a surprise ending.

COLOR. Human interest is best expressed by anecdotes, quotes, and descriptions to illustrate the key points of the story. Each anecdote, quote, and description should advance the story logically. A quote, for example, should not merely repeat in the speaker's words the sense of what is paraphrased ahead of it; rather, the quote should take the event or thought one step further.

WRITING FOR BROADCAST

News copy for radio and television follows the same basic writing principles as those applied to print journalism, but there are some crucial differences: the style is conversational, the content is more compressed, and the grammar, as Fred W. Friendly has put it, "includes the vocabulary of sounds and dialect of pictures."[10] Broadcast scripts are written to be heard rather than read.

Radio scripts must tell the whole story, except for portions filled by tape-recorded material related to the news development. Television scripts tell only those parts of a story that are not obvious from the images on the screen. These conditions apply whether the writing is for hard news, a feature, or a commentary. Because of the special demands of broadcast writing, the premium on the writer's craft is high.

Conversational Style. Copy is read on the air by a broadcaster. The emphasis, therefore, is on familiar words, short sentences, simple and direct construction. Contraction of words is acceptable. But while broadcast copy should sound natural, it usually is composed more like dramatic dialogue than the way a person ordinarily speaks.

Compression. A broadcast writer may have only 20 seconds to tell a story. This time pressure necessitates sophistication in news judgment and economy of language. The writer must select only those facts that are essential to convey the important elements of the story; and he must express the facts accurately and grammatically in the fewest possible words. Wasted facts and words mean wasted air time which, in aggregate, can mean the loss of a story from a newscast for lack of time.

Clarity. Both the broadcaster and the listener must be considered. Copy must be straightforward, written to be read aloud without risk of stumbling by the announcer. Since the words are heard only once, they must be lucid and clear so that the listener understands them immediately. There is no opportunity for backtracking, as in printed stories.

Sound and Sight. Good broadcast writing does not duplicate the obvious. Selective silence is integral to the technique. A familiar sound can make a point without words to describe it. A television viewer need not be told what is obvious in the film, videotape recording, still photograph, map, or chart shown on the screen. Recited words should complement the sounds and sights, and reinforce them. The function of the broadcast writer is to tie the sounds and sights together into a coherent narrative, adding explanation and elaboration when necessary. This matching process (words behind visuals) is called "voice-over."

Leads. As in print journalism, the opening line is the most important. It should be brief, but generally it should tell what or whom the story is about, set the tone (serious or light), and, if possible, provide some perspective to the development. The best leads deal with the *what, who, when*, or *where*, and leave the more complicated *why* and *how* until later in the report.

Direct, or hard, leads are most common. They generally are used for first reports of major news breaks. Delayed, or soft, leads are appropriate for features or follow-ups on stories previously reported. Delayed leads, with background preceding the latest development, may also be used on complicated stories or events with which listeners are unfamiliar.

Attribution. Sources of information should be identified before the information is given. Attribution should precede quotations so that the listener does not think the broadcaster is making the statement himself (quotation marks are not evident on the air as they are in print).

Some Rules. To facilitate reading on the air, abbreviations should be avoided in copy. Symbols should not be used for such things as *dollar* and *percent*. Dates should be written *July fourth* and *December 25th*. Numbers up to *nine* should be written out, but figures can be used for 10 through 999. *Thousand, million,* and *billion* should be written out: for example, *6-million, 124-thousand, seven* rather than 6,124,007.

EDITING THE NEWS

All written material, however good it is to start with, can be improved by sharp editing. In the news business, prevention of errors is particularly important. Credibility is the news organization's stock in trade, and any slump in trust means a slump in customers.

The writer is primarily responsible for the merits of his own copy, and he should go over it before he turns it in. Usually this is not enough. The reporter/writer often is so close to his story that he may miss an error of fact or judgment, or fail to clarify a point, or put the story in proper perspective. The likelihood of such defects is inherent in the news process because of the speed with which newspapers and newscasts are compiled. For these reasons, news organizations have copy editors who perform critical, though largely unheralded, chores.

Whether he works for a newspaper, magazine, or broadcast station, the copy editor stands between the reporter/writer and the public. He is the final check on the content and form of the news. His function is not only to protect against error and distortion, but also to improve the style and substance—and yet preserve as much as possible the words and intent of the original writer. The print copy editor also writes the headlines and, in some organizations, the picture captions. To do all this competently and consistently, the copy editor must be well rounded in knowledge and alert and organized in practice.

Although the introduction of computers and electronic terminals to the newsroom has altered the mechanics of how the copy editor carries out his responsibilities, the responsibilities themselves remain unchanged.

The Copy Desk. The copy editor, or deskperson, is a member of a team called, in aggregate, the "copy desk." At large newspapers and broadcast stations there may be three separate desks that handle, respectively, local, national, and foreign news. The copy editor sits on the "rim" of a horseshoe-shaped table; his immediate boss, called the copy chief or "slotman," sits at the center of the inside curve of the table, known as the "slot." At smaller papers and stations, one group of editors usually handles all copy and its work is done at regular desks.

The head of the copy desk receives all stories, reads them quickly in turn, and assigns each to a copy editor. In assigning the stories, the chief takes into account the editors' speed, headline-writing skills, and special expertise in such fields as politics, culture, and science. Most deskpeople give their stories a quick reading for content and structure, then go through them a second time for close editing. When the editing and headlines are finished, the stories go back to the chief who either approves them for sending to the composing room or returns them for further work.

Essentially the copy editor does what the writer is supposed to do in the first place: make the finished story accurate, readable, concise, forceful, complete. His main duties include the following:

NEWS JUDGMENT. The copy editor exercises news judgment in several ways. Drawing on his knowledge of how a news story is properly constructed, he double-checks the lead to affirm that it hits the theme clearly and grabs the reader or listener. Then he makes sure that the body of the story develops logically and naturally out of the lead. He considers whether the story needs additional background or explanation to make it clearer, or to give it better perspective in relation to the flow of other news. Without distorting or suppressing facts, he may change some of the language to "tone down" or "spruce up" a story. Finally, the editor checks for editorializing and biased and libelous material, and makes certain that the story is balanced, with all views in a controversy represented.

If the copy editor feels that any major textual change is necessary, he should consult first with his supervisory editor and then with the writer of the story. Because the writer knows the story best, he should make any major changes in the copy. The copy editor's role is to be critical, not creative.

CORRECTING ERRORS. Every fact should be verified; those that are questioned by the copy editor and cannot be verified should be deleted. As Garst and Bernstein point out in *Headlines and Deadlines*, mistakes occur most frequently in dates, locations, and the characterization or description of past events. The familiar rule is, "If in doubt, leave it out."

SPELLING AND PUNCTUATION. All long and obscure words should be checked for spelling, and the copy editor should be alert for commonly misspelled words such as "harass" and "accommodate." Proper punctuation promotes clarity, and special attention should be given to the placement of commas and quotation marks.

WORD USAGE AND GRAMMAR. The language should be common, familiar to the audience at which the information is directed. Clichés and jargon should be eliminated. If unfamiliar technical, literary, or colloquial terms cannot be avoided, the copy editor must make sure that they are explained.

The copy editor also must watch for common grammatical mistakes, such as improper sequence of tenses, disagreement in number (singular and plural) between subject and verb, incorrect combinations of pronouns and antecedents, and dangling participles.

STYLE. To minimize confusion in both the processing and the reading of the news, all news organizations have their own typographical styles for abbreviations, capitalization, book and play titles, and spelling of certain words. Maintaining uniformity of style is part of the copy editor's function.

TIGHTENING AND CUTTING. The copy editor is the vigilante for trimming unnecessary words and repetitions. He also is the person who eliminates details and color if a story must be shortened to fit an allocated space. While performing these chores, he should make sure that the sentences are simple and direct, and that the paragraphing is correct.

To indicate the changes he wants when the copy is set in type, the copy editor uses special symbols, writing them in the copy where errors occur. To indicate needed changes in copy already set in type, a proofreader uses many of the same symbols, writing them in the margin of the proof: See page 192.

SYMBOLS USED BY PROOFREADERS

Start paragraph
   or
Start paragraph

Use a line, delete words
to run in words., De-
lete and Do the same
for sentences.

Insert a phrase (word or,)

Insert a mising letter

Insert a comma,

Insert a period.

Take out once letter

Take out some word

Join letters in word

Join words together

Separate these words

Capitalize new york

Make this Lower case

Delete this line

Transpose words two

Transpose the letters

Make fifteen figures

Spell out 8

Abbreviate avenue

Spell out abbrev.

Indicate italics

Indicate bold face

Mark centering

STET
Ignore this correction
....

more of this is coming

or 30 means the end

Add quotation marks

Some edited copy would look like this:

President Carter talked about trade surpluses, the
dollar and ~~general~~ world economic and political
conditions with prime Minister Takeo fukuda of
Japan today, and heard about Japan's plans to
accelerate purchases from the (u.S.) ⊗

   Though Mr. Carter told reporters that the
③ hours of meetings, including a working lunch,
"went well," neither the japanese nor the Americans completely were satisfied with the ~~outcome~~ ⊗ (STET)

(more)

Headlines. The purpose of the newspaper headline is to attract
the reader's attention and tell him at a glance what he can
expect to learn from the accompanying story. In broadcasting,
the same purpose is served by the news capsules included in
quick roundups that often precede full newscasts. The print
headline also serves to create an appealing page typographically,
and, by its relative size, grades the news symbolically.

In the early days of newspapers, the headline was merely a
label that characterized a story in broad terms; the modern
headline, however, makes a statement that captures the essence
of the story.

There are many variations of headlines, depending on the
nature of the story and the paper. Hard-news stories require a
straightforward statement; feature stories can take a bright play
on words. The *New York Times* leans to the serious and straightforward; the *Daily News* emphasizes the bright and punchy.
Despite such diversity, all headlines have a common characteristic: They are confined to a limited space. Thus, the headline
writer must not only be concerned with telling the story, but
he also must do so in words that fit the allotted space.

Headlines come in different shapes and sizes. A head set in large display type that stretches across several columns is called a "banner." Heads on one or two columns can have several parts: a "top," which is the main part that states the primary point of the story; subordinate "decks" or "banks" that elaborate on the top; and "crosslines," which separate the top and the decks and emphasize a secondary theme. Newspaper offices have headline schedules, which are followed by copy editors: If, for example, a story is assigned a "B" head, the deskman knows how many lines he must write and how many space units are available per line (this is determined by the column width and the typeface used for the "B" head).

Some rules and tips for writing headlines:

1. Write the headline *after* editing the story. There are two reasons for this sequence: First, the editing provides a clear gist of the story needed for writing the head; and second, since the story is already edited, the remaining material is not likely to be cut and therefore can be used as the basis for a head.

2. Reduce the story to the bare essentials to determine the kernel of news that should constitute the head. The kernel may not necessarily be in the lead paragraph. To make this determination, ask what the story really means, what stands out, what is different about the story, what might interest the reader.

3. Use the present tense, which connotes immediacy.

4. Avoid editorializing and libelous material.

5. Omit nonessential words, such as articles—a practice designed to economize on space. Keep a synonym guide handy: for example, "compete" might not fit but "vie" would; "decrease" might be too long but "dip" would not.

6. Be specific and direct, and use the active voice.

7. Avoid negatives and repetition.

8. Avoid abbreviations, except for those commonly used such as "Dr." or the "U.S." Abbreviation of the unfamiliar leads to confusion.

9. Every part of a head should have a verb, and parts of a verb should not be separated between lines. For example, the phrase "has not begun" should not be separated "has not" and "begun."

10. Likewise, do not separate an adjective and the word it

modifies, or a preposition and its object (that is, do not end a line with a preposition).

11. Be precise in counting word units. Type will not stretch, and a "broken" head (one that is too long for the space) causes inconvenient and expensive delay because it must be rewritten. Different letters have different widths, and capital letters in general are wider than small letters. Most letters are counted as one unit, but *M* and *W* are wider than normal and *I* is thinner than normal. Most punctuation marks are considered to be a half unit each, as is the space between words.

The trick to making heads fit, then, is to study a unit-count chart, consult a headline schedule to determine the maximum count for the designated head, and count accurately the unit combinations of the words used.

NOTES

1. William Strunk, Jr., and E. B. White, *The Elements of Style,* rev. ed. (New York: The Macmillan Company, 1972), p. 10.

2. *Ibid.,* p. 15.

3. *Ibid.,* p. 17.

4. Robert R. Rathbone, *Communicating Technical Information* (Reading, Mass.: Addison-Wesley Publishing Co., 1972), pp. 64–65.

5. John Hohenberg, *The Professional Journalist* (New York: Holt, Rinehart and Winston, Inc., 1969), p. 85.

6. Melvin Mencher, *News Reporting and Writing* (Dubuque, Iowa: Wm. C. Brown Company Publishers, 1977), p. 56.

7. *Ibid.,* p. 58.

8. *Ibid.,* p. 112.

9. Daniel R. Williamson, *Feature Writing for Newspapers* (New York: Hastings House, Publishers, 1975), p. 12.

10. Edward Bliss, Jr., and John M. Patterson, *Writing News for Broadcast* (New York: Columbia University Press, 1971), p. vii.

SUGGESTED READING

Bernstein, Theodore M. *The Careful Writer: A Modern Guide to English Usage.* New York: Atheneum, 1965.

Bliss, Edward J., and Patterson, John M. *Writing News for Broadcast.* New York: Columbia University Press, 1971.

Garst, Robert E., and Bernstein, Theodore M. *Headlines and Deadlines.* New York: Columbia University Press, 1961.

Mencher, Melvin, *News Reporting and Writing*. Dubuque, Iowa:
Wm. C. Brown Company Publishers, 1977.

Rivers, William L. *The Mass Media: Reporting, Writing, Editing*. New York: Harper & Row, 1975.

Strunk, William, Jr., and White, E. B. *The Elements of Style*.
Rev. ed. New York: The Macmillan Company, 1972.

11

How the News Is Interpreted

It is no longer enough for the journalist simply to chronicle the news; now he also must interpret it. People are not satisfied with knowing only *what* happened; they also want to know *how* and *why* it happened, what it means, and what may happen as a result.

Interpretation of the news is not new, but it has increased steadily since World War II with the growth in the complexity of daily living. To interpret the news requires special skills, knowledgeability, and responsibility. News interpreters are opinion molders, and the specialists are the editorial writers, columnists, and broadcast commentators.

DEFINITION OF INTERPRETATION

"News interpretation" is an imprecise term that can suggest different things to different people, but its broad definition is clear. Interpretive writing adds judgment to straight reporting of the news. It clarifies, analyzes, and explains as well as informs. It tells why an event happened and relates it to other events in a broad context. It indicates the event's meaning by measuring the possible effects. Depth and investigative stories include interpretation. So do editorials and commentaries.

Interpretive writing differs from editorial writing in that it stops short of advocating what should be done about the news. Editorialization, while clarifying and explaining, also includes opinion, states a choice, and seeks to persuade the reader to a specific course of action. Commentary includes opinion.

The late Lester Markel, long-time Sunday editor at the *New York Times* and an early and insistent proponent of interpretive news writing, said the following about interpretation and opinion:

> To report that Spiro Agnew attacks the press is news.
> To explain why Spiro Agnew makes the attack is interpretation.
> To assert that Spiro Agnew is a "radic-unlib" is opinion.
> Interpretation is an objective (as objective as human judgment can be) judgment based on knowledge and appraisal of the situation —good information and sound analysis; it reveals the deeper sense of the news, providing setting, sequence, above all, significance. . . . Opinion, on the other hand, is a subjective judgment and should be confined to the editorial page of newspapers and distinctly labeled on television and radio broadcasts.[1]

GROWTH OF INTERPRETATION

Interpretation began to creep into the press in the World War I years when it became evident that the American people had little understanding of the causes of the war. In 1923 *Time* magazine introduced a new broad approach to the news that included backgrounding and interpreting it. Many newspapers added interpretive columns and commentaries by experienced journalists, usually writing about politics and government in Washington. The complex economic and social programs of the New Deal in the early 1930s encouraged expanded interpretation, and World War II brought the radio commentaries of H. V. Kaltenborn, Lowell Thomas, and Edward R. Murrow.

Since World War II, with the increasing size and complexity of government and society's institutions, interpretive news writing has become a fixture. Special newspaper sections, such as the *New York Times* Sunday "Week in Review," and magazines such as *Harper's*, the *Atlantic, New Republic,* the *Nation, National Review,* and the weekly newsmagazines now regularly publish interpretive articles about business, politics, medicine, religion, education, law, the modern arts, and the social and natural sciences.

Two factors helped speed the growth of interpretive journalism. First, as a result of improved transportation and communications, there is a continuing increase in "knowable" news about people, places, and things. And second, because of expanded education, more people are demanding more information about what is happening around them—and why.

TYPES OF INTERPRETIVE STORIES

Interpretation is found in two basic types of news stories. One is the straight news story that weaves in interpretation with the news. The other is the supplementary "sidebar" that accompanies a straight news story and is intended to put the news development in a broad perspective.

An example of the first type was printed on the front page of the *New York Times* on September 30, 1977, when a court ruled that the supersonic Concorde jetliner, controversial because of its noise, could land in New York. Following are the opening paragraphs of the story, written by Richard Witkin:

A three-judge Federal panel in Manhattan yesterday upheld a lower-court decision to remove the ban on flights of the supersonic Concorde jetliner to Kennedy International Airport.

In its decision, the United States Court of Appeals for the Second Circuit agreed with the lower-court opinion that the 18-month-old ban by the Port Authority of New York and New Jersey was unreasonable and discriminatory, and therefore illegal. It called the case one in which "a technological advance was in imminent danger of being studied into obsolescence" and involved unwarranted official action.

But it modified the lower-court ruling in opening the door for local authorities to reimpose the ban if they could devise noise criteria for Kennedy that did not discriminate against the Concorde.

The Port Authority, which operates the airport, announced that it would appeal the issue to the United States Supreme Court. It said, too, that it would ask that the ban be kept in effect pending the outcome of the appeal.

The prevailing view among legal experts was that a stay keeping the ban in effect would be granted, but that the Supreme Court would quickly refuse to hear the case. That would end the stay and remove the existing ban. Then the way would be open for Concorde flights to begin.

The experts also thought it highly doubtful that there was any way to design noise standards in the foreseeable future that could keep out the Concorde without also barring scores of the older, and therefore noisier, subsonic jetliners.[2]

The last two paragraphs of the excerpts above are interpretation. They explain the meaning of the court's ruling, and suggest what the effects of the action might be.

An example of an interpretive "sidebar" was published by the *Times* earlier in its Sunday "Week in Review" section. The story was written by John Noble Wilford, director of science news for the *Times*, when the Secretary of Transportation decided to permit the Concorde to fly into Washington and New York (a decision that was challenged in court). Headlined "Is Infinite Speed Really an Imperative?" the story put the Concorde controversy into the historical perspective of man's natural urge to do bigger and better—and faster—things. The full text is included below because it illustrates how an interpretive story is built block by block and can be interesting as well as informative.

James Thurber took an ironic view of his fellow man's fascination with the kind of speeds that were leading inexorably to supersonic. He wrote: "Man is flying too fast for a world that is round. Soon he will catch up with himself in a great rear-end collision and Man will never know that what hit him from behind was Man."

But Thurber also created Walter Mitty, man repressed, searching for fulfillment (i.e., adventure and achievement) wherever he could find it, if only in his dreams. Who could not identify with Walter Mitty? He was the kind of man who would chase his tail around the world, if he could—and, in a sense, now he can.

Such is man's growing ambivalence toward the speed and power he has achieved through technology. He follows his instincts to build and create, to extend himself by going faster, higher and farther. Then he is faced with the question, raised in awe and dread, of what to do with his creation, to let it be or to pull back, as in the case of the supersonic transport.

It sometimes seems, for example, that there is an unquenchable human need to fly as fast as possible. Call it a biological imperative, if you will. Any pilot will tell you that speed and the surge of power can be exhilarating. Fighter pilots in World War II would often go a little out of their way to fly through or alongside clouds, which gave them a greater feeling of speed than if they were cruising in open skies.

Speed, moreover, has come to be a metaphor for progress, and in the centuries since the Renaissance, few Westerners have doubted the worth of progress—at least not until recent years. The first mail coach in England in 1784 averaged a mere 10 miles an hour, the first locomotive in 1825, only 13 miles an hour. Then there were 100-mile-an-hour trains by World War II, postwar rocket planes going 4,000 miles an hour, moonbound Apollos at 24,000 miles an hour.

Speed also is a corollary to the human urge to encompass and conquer new worlds, an urge that fueled the great explorations and the Scientific Revolution. This was expressed forcefully at the climax of the H. G. Wells film "Things to come":

"For man there is no rest and no ending. He must go on—conquest beyond conquest. This little planet and its winds and ways, and all the laws of mind and matters that restrain him. Then the planets about him, and at last across immensity to the stars. And when he has conquered all the deeps of space and all the mysteries of time—still he will be but beginning."

Another force behind the supersonic transport could well be a technological imperative. Because something can be done, it will be done.

When rockets and computers came into being, people realized that with them they could explore space, and so they did. When military craft were built to fly faster than the speed of sound, the engineers saw no reason not to apply their talents to a commercial plane with similar speeds. Thus, technology tends to feed on itself, a new technology making more technology possible.

This was undoubtedly a factor in the decisions made in the 1960s by Britain, France, the Soviet Union, and the United States to develop commercial supersonic transports. It had certainly not been demonstrated that there was a clear need to shave by two or three hours the flying time between Europe and the United States or that there was certain economic gain for airlines flying the SST.

An important facet to the technological imperative is the pressure, for military, economic and prestige reasons, to keep a nation's corps of scientists and engineers active and creative. It has been pointed out that 90 per cent of all the scientists who ever lived are alive today—and the way many of them and their engineering colleagues can stay busy is through high-technology projects in aerospace.

This has been suggested as a primary motive behind the British-French venture. Despite costs that their economies could ill afford, the two nations saw in the SST a means of reasserting their claims as major technological powers and of regaining a larger share of the world's aviation market.

Similar reasons were offered to support the United States SST project before it was cancelled by Congress in 1971. In the American case, there was the additional pressure for SST as a means of taking up slack in the aerospace industry after the phasing out of the Apollo Project.

The American decision to abandon the supersonic competition represents a historic break in the tradition of Yankee ingenuity and the Western idea of progress. Transportation Secretary William T. Coleman's decision last week to permit the Concorde to fly into Washington and New York only on a 16-month trial basis illustrates the more critical approach now being taken toward new technologies.

But do our technological imperatives still remain too imperative? In an essay on humanism and science, Dr. Robert L. Sinsheimer, a biologist at the California Institute of Technology, raised the disturbing question:

"Do we really have the freedom on this small planet to choose our technology? Is there a technological imperative, an innate entelechy that determines the course of technological evolution for which men are the unwitting pawns, much as the cells in a developing organism?

"The horror in Mary Shelley's tale, Frankenstein, was not so much that Frankenstein's creation turned out to be a monster but that once created he could not be destroyed. Is this a parable for our science and technology? We can certainly hope not."

The supersonic transport, along with other awesome technologies, like nuclear power and genetic engineering, is perhaps a symbol of a re-emerging imperative: Look very carefully before leaping. Because something can be done, it does not necessarily follow that it must be done; and it should not, in any case, be done without considerable thought.[3]

The Wilford story addressed questions raised by opponents of the supersonic: Why spend all that money, just to cut the trans-Atlantic flying time by two or three hours? What's the hurry? Why pollute the air with all that noise around the airports? To provide some answers, Wilford required a knowledge of history, of science and technology, of psychology, of literature, of the economics of commercial aviation. The story made only glancing reference to the news development (Coleman's decision) because the accompanying straight news story dealt fully with that.

WRITING INTERPRETATION

Interpretive writing usually has special characteristics that are illustrated clearly in the Wilford story. The tendency is to have a delayed lead; that is, the writer "backs into" the story with an anecdote, example, quote, or situation description before mentioning the news to which the story is related. But the theme of the story should be indicated, even if it's just in passing. Wilford used the quotation approach but was careful to mention "supersonic" as a clue to the theme.

If the theme is not stated fully in the lead, it should be established immediately after the opening. Wilford did so with Mitty, "man repressed, searching for fulfillment." Once laid out, the theme should be explained, step by step, and documented with specific facts and figures, examples, quotes from experts, studies. A common technique to provide perspective is the comparison of the current event with another. Wilford compared the supersonic with the mail coach, the train, the World War II airplane, the spaceship.

By its nature, interpretive writing can be solemn, even dull. The good writer livens the story with apt descriptions, metaphors, and literary touches. He follows general statements with explanations or examples. When, for example, Wilford stated that there seems to be an unquenchable human need to fly as fast as possible, he described how pilots like to fly through or alongside clouds.

Because interpretation usually covers a long time span and packs in much information, the writing must be compact. Situations are characterized by phrases rather than descriptive detail. "Speed also is a corollary to the human urge to encompass and conquer new worlds, an urge that fueled the great explorations and the Scientific Revolution"—the phrase captures accomplishments whose descriptions have filled volumes.

Patterns of interpretive writing vary according to the type of story, but the classic organization has this basic form:

1. A lead stating the event or revelation, and putting the news in some broader context; if the lead backs into the story, it should at least allude to the news or the story theme.

2. Elaboration of the context: that is, putting the event in historical perspective, or relating it to a current trend.

3. Balanced explanation of the theme, including conflicting views.

4. A look ahead, based on expert opinion, that suggests the possible effects of the event, the next steps in the trend, or options for solutions if the event poses problems.

If the writer is an expert in the field, like Wilford, he can size up the situation himself. If he is not an expert, he consults an authoritative source—or probably four or five. Usually one explanation is not enough, because good interpretive writing provides all the pros and cons and options.

Most interpretive writers are specialists who follow developments in their field closely. They scan 20 to 30 technical and professional publications regularly. They maintain good and continual contacts with many expert sources, and can consult with them by telephone whenever information is needed quickly. They have their own clippings files and special reference books.

THE THINKING PROCESS

Advance thinking is as important as the actual writing in producing worthwhile interpretation. A small and isolated idea, subjected to chain-link thinking, often grows into a broad concept with wide application and meaning. The curious and imaginative interpretive writer asks himself: What's behind that idea? What other ideas does it suggest? What does it mean to people? What does it tell about people? What can people do with it? What effect could it have on people? What would the average reader like to know about the idea?

How the thinking process works can be illustrated by a story about elephants that appeared under "Ideas and Trends" in the "Week in Review" section of the *New York Times*.

Skimming through an obscure publication for scientists, a writer came upon a report of a study of elephants in Kenya. The principal finding: Elephants don't sweat. Fascinating! What does it tell about elephants? About other animals? About people who live near the elephants? About the environment in which the elephants and people live? The writer plunged into research. He phoned a university in British Columbia to talk to the ecologists who conducted the study. Then he phoned other experts on elephants and Africa. Following is the story that resulted:

> Elephants are having an increasingly difficult time surviving the heat of their tropical habitats because the shade and water on which they rely to keep cool are disappearing, a study has found. Unlike humans, elephants do not sweat as a means of reducing body heat.
>
> Like all mammals, elephants are homoiotherms, which means they maintain a more or less stable body temperature. As with humans, the tissues, especially those of the brain, can withstand only a limited rise in body temperature, approximately nine degrees, before death occurs.
>
> In a study of elephants in Kenya, ecologists Peter Hiley and David Robertshaw found that the animals are poorly equipped physiologically for life in hot climates. Their gray skins tend to absorb the sun's heat. To compensate, elephants seek the shade of trees, wallow in mud, and spray themselves with water.
>
> But as Mr. Hiley points out in a report in the journal *Natural History*, the sources of shade and water are decreasing. A growing human population is reducing the elephants' habitats, and expansion of farming is turning woodlands into grasslands. Without tree cover, land erodes and rainwater, instead of soaking in, runs off.[4]

POLLS AND COMPUTERS

Two social-science techniques that increasingly are factors in the journalistic thinking process are public opinion polls and use of computer data. While public opinion polls have been around for years, they have assumed greater importance since television has emphasized them in forecasting election results. Computers are being used for record analysis that, in most cases, would be too time-consuming and expensive if done manually.

Polls. The traditional and most common polls are those taken by commercial companies, with the findings picked up and used by the press. However, in recent years many newspapers have begun taking their own surveys, either by telephone or by mailed questionnaire. The purpose is to learn what people are thinking about issues and conditions of life. The findings are then incorporated into interpretive stories.

Most newspapers and broadcast stations use poll findings mainly at election time. However, larger papers such as the *New York Times* run their own surveys on social and political issues. The *Charlotte Observer* conducted a mail and telephone survey among area teachers to learn the impact of desegregation on their students, their schools, and themselves. The results provided unusual insight into the local school system.

Some editors are wary of polls because of possible error and misleading distortions. The National Council on Public Polls has cited seven elements that a journalist should ascertain before publishing a poll's findings:

1. Who paid for the poll.
2. When the poll was taken.
3. How the interviews were obtained.
4. How the questions were worded.
5. Who was interviewed.
6. The size of the sample.
7. The base of the data if based on part of a total sample.[5]

Computers. The media use computers to process and analyze data taken from records, largely government records, as a means of investigation. How the technique works is illustrated by two examples:

In 1975 the *Washington Post* published a series of stories based on a three-month study of the U.S. Senate's committee system. The *Post* used its data-processing staff and IBM computer facilities to examine what the committees were spending, where they were spending it, and how they were spending it. The newspaper concluded that many members and employees of committees were misusing the system, often illegally.[6]

The same year the *Knickerbocker News* in Albany, New York, used a computer to investigate and analyze Albany County's tax situation. After processing 95,700 pieces of information from delinquent tax records, the newspaper found that the county was "in the hole for a staggering $9 million."

Commenting on the investigation, executive editor Robert G. Fishenberg wrote:

This new technique, precision journalism, provides an unparalleled ability to undertake penetrating, complex investigative reporting projects involving compilation and study of vast amounts of information in a relatively short time. Such projects would have been impractical, if not impossible, before the age of the computer.[7]

EDITORIALS AND COLUMNS

The most obvious interpretive writing occurs in editorials and columns, which are an integral part of virtually all newspapers, most magazines, and many broadcast stations. The distinguishing feature of editorials and columns is the inclusion of opinion, and thus the writing often is called "opinion writing." The purpose of opinion writing is to stimulate people to think about important events and issues, and to provide leadership for that thinking. Editorials, which generally are unsigned, tend to have an institutional tone, whereas columns carry the byline of the writer and are personal in tone.

Editorials. The properly conducted editorial page has several functions. It serves as a marketplace of ideas by focusing on significant issues and explaining them. It serves as a public voice by promoting specific community or regional interests. By long tradition it serves as a keeper of the public conscience by dealing in moral judgments. It serves as a leader of public opinion by emphasizing the news organization's point of view on the issues discussed.

The editorial page rates low in most readership surveys, but it nevertheless has strong impact on a community's thinking and decisionmaking process. Those who tend to pay closest attention to the editorials, and are most likely to be influenced by them, are government officials and other community leaders.

Although editorials vary in style, organization, and length, most have common characteristics. They usually are pegged to a current news development of general interest. They tend to be short, but some range to 1,000 words or more. They develop a point of view through logical exposition of arguments, and state a conclusion intended to persuade the reader to a course of action. The most effective editorials are written in a clear, concise, direct style. They avoid generalized observations and

opinions; rather, they provide concrete facts and figures based
on solid reporting and research.

On most newspapers the editorials are written by staff members, although "canned" editorials on general subjects can be
purchased from syndicates (obviously, "canned" editorials cannot address local issues of specific communities). On small
papers, the editor, usually in consultation with the publisher,
decides on the subjects to be addressed and writes the editorials
himself. On large newspapers, decisions about subjects and viewpoints to be taken are discussed in daily conferences and the
editorials are written by special writers assigned by the editorial-
page editor.

The *New York Daily News* has a knack for brief, pithy editorials about what it regards as misbehavior in public affairs.
The following was headlined "Ripoff in the Sun":

> More than 5,000 New Yorkers are taking it easy under Florida's
> sunny skies while illegally collecting some $400,000 a week from this
> state's Unemployment Insurance Fund.
>
> Some New Yorkers have it down to a science. When their benefits
> run out, they come back to New York to work for 20 weeks and
> then head back to the land of Disney World for another 39-week
> vacation paid for by New York employers.
>
> New York officials have asked Washington to crack down on the
> fraud, which endangers benefits for honest, unemployed citizens. We
> hope the feds step in right away.
>
> This state's Unemployment Insurance Fund was not designed to
> become a mainstay of Florida's economy.[8]

Columns. Personal commentary in the form of columns comes
from three main sources: staff members of individual news
organizations, syndicated writers who are not attached to any
news organizations, and laymen who submit free-lance material for "op-ed" and opinion pages. Although they are not
columns, letters to the editor are another source of personal
commentary. Most columns deal with public affairs and politics,
but some concentrate on special fields such as religion, medicine,
and education.

Regular columnists produce from one to seven columns a
week, usually between 500 and 1,000 words each. Most of the
better-known columnists are based in Washington and New

York. Some of the more influential columnists are staff members of newspapers, such as James Reston and Tom Wicker of the *New York Times* and David Broder of the *Washington Post*, but their columns are distributed to other papers by their organizations' own syndicates. Some of the most widely circulated columns are by "free-lance" journalists, such as Jack Anderson and Joseph Alsop, whose commentaries are distributed by syndicates to papers across the country.

Because of the monopoly press situation in most cities, newspapers generally try to have a balance, or at least some diversity, of viewpoints on their opinion pages. If the paper's own columnists tend to be "liberal," there is usually a syndicated "conservative" writer represented also. Many papers have added "op-ed" pages in recent years for this purpose, as well as to allow an outlet for laymen's opinions.

Good columns are similar to editorials in their style, organization, and facts-and-figures documentation. The main difference is the emphasis on personal opinion in columns. Some columns simply represent personal reaction to an event. In 1975, Mary McGrory of the *Washington Star* won a Pulitzer Prize for her political commentaries. The following is the beginning of a column, written after President Nixon's last State of the Union message, that was submitted as part of McGrory's Pulitzer nomination:[9]

> The town needed a laugh, heaven knows, but who would have thought that the President, of all people, would provide us with 45 minutes of low comedy in, of all things, his State of the Union message?
>
> Basically, it was situation comedy. Here was a President facing impeachment, waiting for multiple indictments of his closest aides, fighting off a court summons from one of the "two finest public servants" he has ever known, hanging onto his great office by his fingernails.
>
> The heavily made-up man on the podium spoke of himself as a miracle worker.
>
> He has cleaned the air and made peace. He has reduced subsidies. He will bid the waters of recession recede and they will obey. He will heal the sick with a health plan that will not require new taxes.
>
> The only possible reason for turning him out of office, as he told it, would be that he is too good for us.

The column then summarized the main points made by Nixon, and ended with this paragraph:

> The Republicans gave him a standing ovation. If it wasn't a swan song, it was theirs. If he survives to give another January Fantasy, they don't expect to be around to hear it. That was the reality that was carefully blotted out in the chamber. So the Republicans chatted, smiled and clapped for what every last one of them hopes will be Richard Nixon's last State of the Union.

CRITICISM

Criticism, as the word implies, is opinion writing of a special kind. In journalism it generally is applied to the arts: books, theater, opera, concerts, art exhibits, dance, movies. Nowadays, it also extends to television programs. Criticism can be positive as well as negative, and a prestigious critic for a major publication has awesome power in the world of culture: his or her review can mean the difference between success and failure for a book, a play, a movie.

Once relegated to the obscure pages of newspapers and magazines, news of the arts has become increasingly popular and prominent as the public's interest in culture has grown. Critical writing is featured in the new "lifestyle" pages, and many television and radio programs now have special sections for reviews and discussion of the arts. Metropolitan newspapers tend to pay more attention to criticism than do smaller papers on the ground that interest in the arts is generally highest in urban centers.

Most large newspapers and magazines have their own specialists for reviewing and critiquing. Those that do not may give a specific criticism assignment to a reporter with a special interest and aptitude in music or art; or simply use material distributed regularly by the news services and syndicates. In any case, the fundamental requisite for a writer of criticism is expertise in the field.

There are two basic types of criticism: One is the "instant" review of a play or concert for immediate use under deadline pressure; this is the dominant form. The other is the longer critique, written without deadline pressure and used later when the writer has had time for thoughtful analysis; these critiques interpret meanings of events and motivations of the artists involved.

As opinion writing, criticism has characteristics similar to those of editorials and columns. There is no set format, and the writer has considerable freedom of style. Accurate reporting and backgrounding of the plot (only briefly), the performance, and the audience reaction are important. The writer's judgments should be supported by description and explanation, based on specific facts and figures whenever possible. The writing should be balanced—few works are all good or all bad, and a single review can contain elements of both—and the conclusion should flow out of the arguments presented.

While most critical writing is identified with professional works, much of it, especially in smaller cities, is applied to amateur works. It is important that the writer recognize the difference. A performance by the community theatrical group or orchestra should not be judged by the professional standards applied to performances at Lincoln Center in New York.

NOTES

1. Lester Markel, "Interpretive News," *Editor and Publisher*, Aug. 12, 1972, p. 7.
2. Richard Witkin, *New York Times*, Sept. 30, 1977, p. 1.
3. John Noble Wilford, "The Week in Review," *New York Times*, Feb. 8, 1976, p. 1.
4. "Week in Review," *New York Times*, Feb. 22, 1976, p. 9.
5. Stephen Isaacs, "The Pitfalls of Polls," *Columbia Journalism Review*, May/June 1972, pp. 32–33.
6. Isaacs, *Washington Post*, Feb. 16, 1975, p. 1.
7. Robert G. Fishenberg, *Knickerbocker News*, Jan. 13, 1976, p. 1.
8. *New York Daily News*, March 23, 1978, p. 51.
9. Mary McGrory, *Washington Star*, Feb. 3, 1974.

SUGGESTED READING

Charnley, Mitchell V. *Reporting*. New York: Holt, Rinehart and Winston, Inc., 1966.

Hohenberg, John. *The Professional Journalist*. New York: Holt, Rinehart and Winston, Inc., 1968.

MacDougall, Curtis D. *Interpretative Writing*. New York: The Macmillan Company, 1968.

Meyer, Philip. *Precision Journalism*. Bloomington, Ind.: Indiana University Press, 1973.

12

How the News Is Presented

The whole news process reaches a climax with the crucial question: Which stories should be used?

There is an unending flow of news, and thousands of stories are available every day. It is physically impossible for a newspaper or broadcast station to report them all. Someone has to choose which stories should be presented to the public, and the burden falls mainly on anonymous editors in the newsrooms. Their decisions are influenced by a mixture of economic, social, and journalistic factors, including their own tastes and prejudices.

Most of the following discussion relates to newspapers, the primary purveyors of news. For broadcasting, some of the operational factors differ.

SPACE LIMITATIONS

On an average day an average newspaper uses one story out of five it receives, and throws away the rest because it does not have enough space to print them. The ratio of discarded stories on a large metropolitan paper is even higher, perhaps seven to one, because it has more sources of news and more stories to choose from. The percentage is equally high with broadcast stations because only a relatively few stories can be squeezed into the limited air time devoted to news.

What this means to the flow of information to the public is underscored by Ben H. Bagdikian in *The Information Machines*: "It is as though the events reported in 80 percent of the stories that arrive in local newsrooms never happened. This is inevitable but it is awesome."[1]

The bulk of the news stories come from the news services, mainly AP and UPI, which pump a steady stream of words into newsrooms via teletype machines. The wire services, with reporters scattered around the globe, supply stories of every stripe in an attempt to satisfy the diverse needs of their varied customers spread over a wide geographic area. Because of this scattershot approach, only the few big stories of the day have common appeal to a large number of newspapers. Thus a paper typically rejects the majority of stories it receives on the wires. While many of the stories on the competing wires are duplicative, many are not.

Every small daily and broadcast station has at least one of the wire service machines. A medium-sized news organization may have both AP and UPI plus a couple of supplementary news wires. Large metropolitan papers and network newsrooms have a dozen or more. In addition, every news organization has its own reporters constantly adding dozens of local stories to the news reservoir.

The result, studies have shown, is that a typical newspaper on a typical day has perhaps 500 stories from which to choose, and room for 100. The largest metropolitan papers have more than 2,000 news items available, and room for 300.

THE GATEKEEPERS

The journalists who have the responsibility for selecting the stories to be seen by the public are called "gatekeepers" by social scientists because they control the gates that let out the news. The term is applied to those managerial editors whose job it is to scan all the available stories and to judge whether they should be used or tossed in the wastebasket.

Before these local editors go to work, however, preliminary

gatekeepers play an initial role in determining which stories will be available.

Key gatekeepers are the wire service managers and reporters. They decide which news events are worthy of coverage—and to what extent—for their worldwide services to their clients. Stories about these events originate at thousands of points in the United States and abroad and are fed into the wire network. All these stories must be channeled through regional bureaus, which must eliminate or edit much of the material because of the limited capacity of the main wires going to the newspapers. Editors at the relay bureaus thus serve as gatekeepers also.

In the newspaper office there are several gatekeepers. The city, national, and foreign editors make the original decisions on which stories their reporters and correspondents will cover and make available for use. Then, since there is never enough room for all the stories, they decide which of the finished stories will be used and at what length. They are guided by the allocation of space for local, national, and foreign news, as decided by a conference of the executive editors. On small papers the selection process often is carried out by the editor alone.

In addition to the general news, similar decisions must be made for departmental news such as sports, lifestyle, culture, business and finance. Editors of these departments make the selections depending on the space allotted by the executive editors. Space must also be allocated for photographs.

Gatekeepers reach their positions only after much journalistic experience, usually in both reporting and copy editing. The average gatekeeper is in his forties, well educated, and intellectually sharp. He is calm, confident, and capable of quick decisions. To keep abreast of news trends and developments, he regularly reads the leading newspapers and magazines.

THE ADVERTISING FACTOR

The amount of space available for news is largely determined by the advertising department. Advertising gets high priority because it supplies most of the newspaper's income. Depending on the amount of advertising for the day, the advertising department recommends the total number of pages to be printed; columns are then allocated to advertising, and what remains is the news "hole." Some papers have a minimum news "hole" regardless of the amount of advertising. The typical space ratio is 60 percent for advertising, and 40 percent for news, including the departments, although this may vary somewhat.

Space for news depends as much on the American consumer as on the flow of news events. The biggest papers in terms of pages are on Wednesdays, Thursdays, and Fridays because these are the days that families plan their weekend shopping and newspapers have more advertising. More pages for advertising means more space for news.

OTHER FACTORS

Aside from the size of the news "hole," the gatekeepers must consider various other factors in their calculations. Among them are the audience, mechanical requirements, local emphasis, the desired appearance of the paper, and whether the paper comes out in the morning or afternoon.

Audience. Gatekeepers must keep the interests of the readers in mind. The *New York Times*, for example, considers itself a newspaper of record and is read widely by the upper and middle classes, including government officials, diplomats, business people, and scholars. The *Daily News* in New York appeals more to the blue-collar worker. Rural audiences want farm news, while urban readers are more interested in the problems of the cities.

Mechanical Requirements. Newspapers take hours to put together; the mechanisms that convert news into print are cumbersome. At the same time, there are deadlines to meet so that the circulation department can meet strict schedules for planes, trains, trucks, and carriers who distribute the papers. These two factors create an imperative to fill up the back pages of the paper early, even before all of the day's stories are known. And once a story is committed to type, there is a reluctance to replace it with a later story because of the time and money involved.

Local Emphasis. Editors have a built-in prejudice toward using local stories because of reader interest and because they have invested their own effort and manpower in the coverage. Moreover, they figure that many readers get the major national and international news from radio and television.

Appearance and Balance. Typography often determines the

selection of a story. In laying out pages, an editor seeks harmony, unity, and balance of stories, headlines, and pictures. For variety he likes to mix features with straight news stories occasionally, and he tries to keep related news items together. Thus, in considering several stories of equal newsworthiness, he may choose one because of its length or tone.

Morning and Afternoon. Because morning papers are put together mainly after the predictable news events of the day have been completed, the gatekeepers have more time to make their judgments. Because afternoon papers are produced and distributed while the nation's business is still taking place, the gatekeeping decisions must be made hurriedly: developments occur in stories already committed to an afternoon paper, and changes must be made as deadline approaches; or fresh news suddenly develops and must be inserted quickly, displacing earlier stories.

INFLUENCES AND PRESSURES

Within the framework of the established factors, the gatekeeper is subject to a variety of influences and pressures that affect the two broad perspectives from which he approaches his selection role.

First, he is an educator, passing along information that is important for people to know; and, second, he is a popular communicator, under commercial pressure to attract the widest possible audience to his newspaper. Thus, as Bagdikian points out, the gatekeeper is saying two things—that are not necessarily the same: First, "This is what I think you ought to know," and second, "This is what I think will interest you."[2]

Important to the gatekeeper's role is a knowledge of how audiences react to the various media. One study has shown that people select their source of information on the basis of habit, of congruence with their own views, of usefulness to their own lives, and of convenience of availability.[3] Another study has suggested that these bases of selection are generally determined by a person's lifestyle. For example, a young person interested in games, jazz, and unstructured living is likely to read a lively tabloid rather than a serious paper heavy on politics.[4]

A study by RAND, a think tank that specializes in social

sciences, found that gatekeepers, in order to keep up with the flow of stories, must make their decisions very fast. With stories that turned out to be rejects, the average gatekeeper scanned each story only about two seconds before making the decision; with stories that were put aside for possible use in the paper, he spent a little longer. To achieve such speed, the gatekeeper clearly is guided by values, based on influences and pressures, to which he responds automatically.

The starting point for the decisions is the common conception of newsworthiness shared by all professional journalists. The gatekeeper immediately looks for the basic elements of news: timeliness, proximity, conflict, drama, prominence, significance for his specific audience.

To some extent the gatekeeper is influenced by the "wolf pack" psychology. His "herd" instinct impels him to give strong consideration to what others see and hear as "big" news. For example, AP and UPI start off their daily wire transmissions with a list of stories that their editors feel are the day's "big news." Hurried editors tend to pick up these suggestions as the basis for their planning. If a newspaper gatekeeper hears a news story on radio or television, he is likely to give it special consideration in his planning; the same is true of the broadcast gatekeeper who sees a story in the morning paper.

At the same time, the gatekeeper, like other journalists, follows certain professional standards such as accuracy, fairness, objectivity, good taste. These standards are taken for granted throughout the profession, and violation of them is greeted with contempt. In these terms, the individual journalist cares deeply about the reaction of his colleagues to his work. Thus, since there is close association among journalists, one of the most effective influences on gatekeeping is internal.

Another internal influence is the news organization's overall policy as seen by the publisher. This policy is not written down anywhere, and bias in the treatment of news is contrary to the professional standards of journalism; nevertheless, certain management leanings always exist and are known by the staff members. For example, it is not inconceivable that management's feelings about nuclear power plants or Middle East diplomacy as expressed on the editorial page might be reflected in the selection, length, and placement of news stories on these subjects.

External pressures come from important news sources and their press officers, from special-interest groups, from advertisers. All seek to get special attention in the news report. The professionalism of gatekeepers, as well as reporters, militates against submitting to such pressures.

Finally, there are the gatekeeper's own values, feelings, and interests developed over the years. These factors, which often are pivotal in split-second decisions, derive from his geographical origin, family upbringing, educational background, social and political contacts. It would be naïve to assume that journalists have no personal prejudices and preferences and that, consciously or unconsciously, they play no part in his treatment of the news.

SELECTION OF STORIES

Within the general selection process there is the need for appropriate balance among local, national, international, and special-interest news. How much space is allocated to each category depends on the individual news organization, the audience it is trying to reach, and the relative newsworthiness of the stories on a particular day. The larger newspapers, especially along the coasts, tend to carry more national and international stories than do the smaller papers, especially away from the coasts.

Within the space allotments, city, national, and foreign editors have story preferences based on their gatekeeping judgments. These preferences are made known in editorial conferences for overall planning of the day's paper. From the list of potential stories, perhaps a half-dozen must be chosen for the front page. These are crucial decisions, because the front page is the newspaper's "face" in the eyes of most readers.

After the front page has been determined, the remaining stories are chosen in descending order of importance for placement on the inside pages. Articles in special fields, such as business, sports and entertainment, usually are grouped in predictable sections of the paper. The stories are placed by the makeup editor, in consultation with the gatekeeping editors when appropriate, taking into account the mechanical restrictions, the need for page balance typographically, the logic of keeping related items together, the attractiveness of graphics. The planning is subject to adjustment when a late news story breaks, but generally only the front page is affected by last-minute changes.

Although there have been many innovations in newspaper design and makeup, traditional patterns and practices still govern the placement of stories in most papers, particularly on the front page. The most important story usually is placed on the right-hand side (column 8 on an 8-column page) of page 1, above the fold, because that part can be seen when the newspaper is folded on a newsstand.

The rest of the columns are rated in display value as follows: 1 (extreme left side of page) or 6, 3, 7, 5, 4, 3. The trend in makeup is toward fewer than eight columns to a page, but the priority patterns remain the same. The size of the headline and the length of the story also denote the relative importance given a story by the editors.

PRESENTATION IN THE FUTURE

As the use of computers increases, and as home video information centers come into being, the presentation of news will change and the role of gatekeeping editors will become more important. Consumers will be able to pursue subjects beyond the standard daily news report.

Although gatekeepers receive thousands of words across their desks today, in the future machines will be able to put millions of words into their computers. What this will mean to editors is forecast by Bagdikian in *The Information Machines*:

> They will have an audience more knowledgeable and, because of added channels of information, more varied in its specialized interests. And they will have a greatly enlarged number of possibilities from which to choose, requiring greater selectivity. The standard package of news is not likely to expand much in words and video time, so the same quantity of information will have to be selected from a much larger reservoir, and presented in a way compatible with a more knowledgeable audience.[6]

Bagdikian points out that material now discarded by editors and lost can be retained in the computer memory and retrieved at will.

"The editor will have available not only the product of daily reporting and monitoring," Bagdikian notes, "but more specialized articles that appear only in periodicals and books. These, too, will be computerized and in microforms, and will be available to the reporter and editor for reference in compiling the daily package of news, and to the consumer who wishes to see them or portions of them."[7]

NOTES

1. Ben H. Bagdikian, *The Information Machines* (New York: Harper Colophon Books, 1971), p. 90.
2. *Ibid.*, p. 110.
3. W. Phillips Davison, James Boylan, and Frederick T. C. Yu, *Mass Media* (New York: Praeger Publishers, 1976), p. 154.
4. Barbara Bryant, Frederick Currier, and Andrew J. Morrison, "Relating Lifestyle Factors of a Person to His Choice of a Newspaper," *Journalism Quarterly*, Spring 1976, pp. 75–79.
5. Maxwell E. McCombs and John B. Mauro, "Predicting Newspaper Readership from Content Characteristics," *Journalism Quarterly*, Spring 1977, pp. 3–7.
6. Bagdikian, p. 280.
7. *Ibid.*, p. 281.

SUGGESTED READING

Bagdikian, Ben H. *The Information Machines*. New York: Harper Colophon Books, 1971.

Davison, W. Phillips, and Yu, Frederick T. C., eds. *Mass Communications Research*. New York: Praeger Publishers, 1971.

Turnbull, Arthur T., and Baird, Russell N. *The Graphics of Communication*. New York: Holt, Rinehart and Winston, Inc., 1975.

Index